ENDING POVERTY

How People, Businesses, Communities and Nations can Create Wealth from Ground - Upwards

Dominion V. Judah, PhD

Dedication

I dedicate this book to God and to all individuals, families, communities, nations and regions which are living in poverty around the world, especially those who live on less than a dollar per day. Part of my mission to the world is to end poverty and we will make it happen. Meanwhile, the purpose of this book is to educate everyone to play their role as we replace poverty with prosperity for all.

Appreciation

My sincere profound appreciation goes to everyone who has ever contributed to my life and success towards making this book a reality. I love and celebrate you all.

TABLE OF CONTENTS

INTRODUCTION

The problem of eradicating poverty has been one that humanity has battled for ages. The good news is that poverty can be eliminated with the correct strategy and resources. Fighting poverty is not a humanitarian activity; it is a question of justice and a way to help everyone reach their full potential. Even today, the lack of access to food and clean water results in hundreds of deaths daily, and almost 50% of the world's population lives in poverty.

Together, we can eradicate disease, end world hunger, and give everyone a chance to get better off in life. This book will thoroughly investigate how people, corporations, communities, and countries may build wealth from scratch. It will go over tried-and-true methods for assisting folks who are experiencing poverty to break free from their cycle, achieve economic stability, and have a better future. We know individuals' hardships, but how can we abolish poverty worldwide? We may contribute in numerous small ways to the fight against poverty. Although many simple ways exist to prevent poverty, there are only sometimes clear solutions. Don't undervalue even the most minor activities because every little bit helps those in need.

Poverty traps are the result of a confluence of factors, such as a lack of access to credit and capital markets, severe environmental degradation (reducing agricultural production potential), corrupt governance, capital flight, inadequate educational systems, a high prevalence of infectious diseases, a shortage of public healthcare services, conflict, and impaired physical infrastructure.

It is suggested that those living in poverty need to be provided with substantial assistance to build up a critical mass of capital and break out of their situation. This hypothesis sheds light on the potential failure of poverty alleviation efforts that do not give sufficient assistance. Those in need will continue to rely on aid until they build up an adequate capital base, and then they will regress if aid is cut off. Studies have examined the function of additional elements, such as healthcare, in keeping a society mired in the poverty trap. The National Bureau of Economic Research (NBER) discovered that countries with worse health tend to remain stuck in a cycle of poverty despite having similar levels of education as other countries.

Scientists at the University of Florida in Gainesville compiled data on the world's economy and diseases. Researchers found that people in places where human, animal, and crop diseases were less common were more likely to escape poverty independently.

The cycle of guilt must be broken to end poverty. Everyone is aware of and frequently hears about the global poverty crisis. However, a lot of us have given up trying to change it. Every day, people who have the means to aid those in need are disregarded, whether by ignoring street beggars or charity events.

We must stop hiding our guilt and accept responsibility for our acts if we want to make a difference. The central thesis of this book is that creativity and releasing the potential of people and communities are the means through which poverty can be eradicated. It will offer a thorough manual for establishing sustainable means of subsistence, inspiring company owners to launch new ventures, and improving systems for delivering vital services.

We'll examine the role played by the government in eradicating poverty through the reform of public policy, funding for infrastructure, and other social welfare programs. The book will examine the successful policies different countries have implemented worldwide and explain how states might build on their accomplishments. It will examine how international collaboration may promote economic expansion and guarantee equal opportunity for everyone.

The poverty issue can be resolved by raising benefits, generating jobs, granting access to credit to start businesses, or enhancing living conditions. The European Poverty Action Network (EAPN) has identified employment, disability, low education, poor health, belonging to a minority racial or ethnic group, and living in a rural or underdeveloped area as important factors that increase a person's vulnerability to poverty. These are all crucial factors to consider in the fight against poverty. Every person should want to get better and develop. They shouldn't be concerned about a cyclone damaging their homes or about crooked officials or strong corporations stealing them. They require the necessary infrastructure to ensure their influence is felt constantly, not just when they hold protests against poverty. They should have access to basic rights like healthcare and education. Even the environment has an impact. As a result, we understand that poverty may be reduced anywhere and that the country's problems are not unique. The most important thing is to avoid thinking that if millions could raise their daily income to $1.92 (beyond the World Bank's extreme poverty threshold), all problems would be resolved.

This book is intended to serve as a useful toolset that offers ideas and concrete steps to follow. The plain writing style makes it easy for everyone to understand the most recent findings. This book gives you the information and tools you need to influence your community, regardless of whether you are a policymaker, corporate leader, development practitioner, or simply someone who wants to make a difference in the fight to eradicate poverty. Poverty can be eradicated. It is feasible to establish a future where everyone can access economic possibilities to help them escape poverty by comprehending how people, corporations, communities, and nations can create wealth from nothing. The instructions required to make that future reality are included in this book.

CHAPTER ONE
HISTORICAL OVERVIEW

Poverty signifies the absence of adequate resources to guarantee a basic standard of living for oneself and one's family. This entails the insufficiency of access to necessities required for subsistence. Their most fundamental needs can't be addressed because of this. Poor families may need access to safe shelter, adequate nutrition, medical care, and safe drinking water. The poverty threshold and the population counted as poor might vary from country to country. Remember that poverty is a social and economic reality, not just having too little money. Racism, homophobia, transphobia, sexism, and a lack of educational opportunities are all contributors.

Poverty signifies the absence of access to the most fundamental resources required for a dignified existence. The lack of shelter shields from the elements, the absence of sufficient nourishment to sustain health, the deprivation of medical care that preserves life, and the denial of safe drinking water ensures well-being. Poverty, therefore, is not limited to financial paucity; it extends to the very essence of human survival and dignity.

The contours of poverty, however, are not uniform across the globe. They manifest in multifaceted ways, shaped by historical, cultural, and geographical contexts. The thresholds that define poverty in one nation may not resonate in another, unveiling the intricacies of a challenge that defies a one-size-fits-all solution. It is a challenge not isolated within economic brackets; it echoes across societal dimensions, fueled by structural injustices and systemic biases.

Yet, the implications of poverty cascade far beyond its apparent constraints. It echoes through corridors of power, disrupts the social fabric, and perpetuates inequalities that undermine the foundations of justice and human rights. Poverty is not merely a numerical measure but a lens through which we perceive the intricacies of a society's moral compass and ethical priorities.

To be impoverished is to stand at the precipice of exclusion, where the ability to provide for oneself, one's family, and one's community becomes a constant struggle. It is a landscape where the pursuit of necessities becomes an uphill battle, where food, clothing, shelter, and medication, once taken for granted, transform into distant aspirations. Poverty amplifies vulnerability, strips away agency, and condemns individuals to a perpetual survival cycle, leaving little room for growth and empowerment.

However, poverty's impact is not confined to individual lives. It resonates through neighborhoods, shaping the destiny of communities and casting a shadow over generations. The spiral of poverty often engenders societal challenges—crime, unemployment, inadequate education, and deteriorating health. It breeds a vicious cycle, where the absence of resources perpetuates an environment that hinders progress and undermines social cohesion.

This cycle of poverty is not a modern phenomenon; it's a thread that weaves through the annals of history. Ancient civilizations were marred by extreme wealth disparities, where the privileged few basked in opulence while the majority languished in poverty. Feudal systems of the Middle Ages perpetuated this divide, leaving the masses bereft of resources, their lives controlled by the whims of a ruling elite.

The advent of the Industrial Revolution brought about transformative change, yet it also unveiled a new facet of poverty. The burgeoning factories and urban centers provided economic growth but also sowed the seeds of labor exploitation, unsafe working conditions, and a rising tide of child labor. The rural exodus to cities for better opportunities reshaped the urban landscape, highlighting the harsh realities of urban poverty and overcrowded living conditions.

This narrative was not confined to Europe; it resonated across continents. America, while a land of promise, also harbored poverty amidst prosperity. Colonial settlers grappled with subsistence living, and the Industrial Revolution introduced its challenges. The Great Depression of the 1930s plunged millions into abject poverty, starkly underscoring the fragility of economic stability.

In response to these socio-economic challenges, nations began to craft safety nets. Social welfare systems emerged to alleviate poverty's grip, offering a glimmer of hope through education, employment opportunities, and assistance programs. The latter half of the 20th century saw progress in the United States as government interventions and policies significantly dropped poverty rates.

However, as the world progressed, the challenges of poverty persisted. Obstacles such as racial biases, unequal access to education, and limited job opportunities continued to cast a shadow. The persistent issue of poverty prompted societies to reckon with the structural injustices perpetuating inequality, inspiring a renewed commitment to equitable progress.

In the developing world, poverty's grip remains particularly stark. Economic disparities between affluent and struggling nations exacerbate the divide, leaving millions vulnerable to relentless scarcity. Regions like Sub-Saharan Africa grapple with limited healthcare access, inadequate job prospects, and the cyclical nature of poverty, which continues to undermine efforts toward development.

The nation's focused efforts have lifted millions from the clutches of poverty through a multi-pronged approach. By empowering citizens with education, healthcare, and economic opportunities, China's transformation is a testament to the potential for progress when comprehensive strategies are implemented.

Yet, the challenge of eradicating poverty is not confined to a single nation; it is a global endeavor. Governments, non-profit organizations, and individuals are vital players in this symphony of change. Policies such as minimum wages, social safety nets, and healthcare initiatives form the foundation of a more equitable society. Collaboration and determination underpin efforts to transition from aid dependency to self-sufficiency, ultimately breaking the cycle of poverty.

The history of poverty underscores its pervasive nature and the possibilities for change. It's a story that spans epochs, civilizations, and geographies—a reminder that the struggle for human dignity is universal. This deprivation narrative also kindles hope, for a world without poverty is attainable with the right policies, partnerships, and determination.

As we envision a future devoid of poverty's grip, we must recognize that the path forward is not uncharted. Innovations, collaborations, and determined action can create a world where every individual's basic needs are met. Education, healthcare, and economic opportunities are not mere aspirations but the building blocks of a society where prosperity is accessible.

However, the challenge has its complexities. Poverty's roots are often traced to systemic barriers, historical injustices, and institutional biases. Therefore, eradicating poverty necessitates a comprehensive approach that dismantles inequalities, empowers communities, and fosters an environment where individuals can survive and thrive.

China's experience, although inspiring, also highlights the significance of adopting a nuanced approach. The process of relocating citizens from rural to urban areas, coupled with providing opportunities, gives rise to inquiries regarding social integration and the preservation of culture. Poverty is not a riddle to be solved with a singular solution; rather, it is a multi-faceted challenge that demands customized strategies founded upon empathy, pragmatism, and a profound comprehension of local dynamics.

In a more interconnected world than ever, the fight against poverty is a shared responsibility. Global institutions, policymakers, businesses, and civil society all play a pivotal role in shaping a future where poverty is relegated to history books. The United Nations' Sustainable Development Goals set forth a roadmap for ending poverty in all its forms, acknowledging that eradicating poverty is intrinsically linked to broader social and economic progress.

China's success story demonstrates that progress is possible when a nation takes a proactive stance driven by the collective will to uplift its citizens. This spirit of collective action is not unique to China; it is a sentiment that resonates across cultures, borders, and societies. Whether through government initiatives, community-led efforts, or international partnerships, the fight against poverty is a testament to humanity's capacity for transformation.

In the grand scheme of history, poverty's narrative continues to evolve. It's a story that reminds us of our shared humanity, our interconnectedness, and our responsibility to leave no one behind. As we look to the future, let us channel the lessons of the past to shape a world where every individual has the opportunity to thrive. Let us break the cycle of poverty, weave a new equity narrative, and create a legacy of progress for generations to come.

Social and Political Influences

Across time, the specter of poverty has loomed large, a product of intricate interplays between society's dynamics and the wielding of political power. This complex narrative of deprivation has been woven through the ages, shaped by myriad social and political influences that have left an indelible mark on the destinies of nations and individuals alike. The historical backdrop of poverty is painted with the hues of inequality, unequal resource distribution, and economic disparity, all of which have been contended, contemplated, and transformed by the ebb and flow of human thought and governance.

In antiquity, the origins of poverty were often attributed to the unequal distribution of resources and wealth. Ancient societies viewed it as a consequence of an imbalanced allocation of societal riches. This perspective, resonating through the corridors of time, was embraced by Enlightenment philosophers, who postulated that economic inequality was a natural precursor to poverty. Their musings, carried on the wings of reason, called for interventions to draw the government into the fray, suggesting that aid and welfare programs could be instruments of change in the battle against poverty.

The evolution of this viewpoint paralleled the transformative journey of the 19th century, a period defined by the Industrial Revolution's mechanized embrace. Here, poverty's canvas expanded to encompass the nuances of personal accountability. Politicians of the era looked beyond societal assistance, urging individuals to chart their course out of poverty's clutches. The realm of self-sufficiency became a beacon of hope, a clarion call to rise above circumstances and transform one's fate through individual endeavor.

Amid this ideological mosaic emerged Charles Booth, a voice that would resonate across time. Booth's perspective, rooted in the conviction that poverty was inextricably linked to the absence of ambition and education, heralded a perspective that echoed across generations. His views gained currency, paving the way for an era where personal empowerment became synonymous with emancipation from poverty's grasp.

Poverty, however, did not remain static. The cataclysmic Great Depression in the 1930s shattered economies, engendering mass impoverishment and forcing societies to reevaluate their stance. Governments, faced with the urgency of the moment, turned to direct assistance as a means to stem the tide of suffering. Initiatives such as Social Security in the United States and European unemployment insurance sought to provide a safety net for those ensnared by economic turmoil.

Yet, this evolution was far from linear. The pendulum of perception swung once more as the mid-20th century arrived. The civil rights movement, women's liberation, and anti-poverty organizations emerged as catalysts for change. This era saw the inception of government assistance programs like food stamps and Medicaid in the United States, forging a path toward addressing the material symptoms of poverty. However, the deeper-rooted issues, the social and economic underpinnings perpetuating poverty, remained elusive, demanding attention beyond the surface.

In the backdrop of these historical currents, the present continues to bear the weight of poverty's legacy. Governments persist in alleviating suffering through welfare mechanisms, yet they have expanded their purview to encompass education and employment opportunities. On a global scale, international bodies such as the World Bank and the United Nations have marshaled microfinance and debt relief strategies in the ongoing battle against poverty's grip.

The symphony of poverty's evolution serves as a testament to the profound impact of social and political variables on its presence, persistence, and distribution. The intricate dance of society's structure and the wielding of political power has shaped the contours of poverty and determined who bears its weight and who manages to transcend its clutches. The narrative of poverty thus emerges not as an isolated tale of scarcity but as a mirror reflecting the intricacies of human societies and their engagement with power.

As we navigate the complexities of addressing poverty in our time, it becomes imperative to contextualize our efforts within this historical continuum. Governments' roles in mitigating suffering and fostering development are integral, but the story of poverty extends far beyond welfare programs. It intertwines with the very fabric of society, enmeshed with issues of justice, inequality, and the distribution of resources.

The chapters of history unveil the extent of what has been accomplished, but they also beckon us to push further. Understanding poverty as a multifaceted challenge, intertwined with the intricate dance of social structures and political will, urges us to go beyond surface solutions. It impels us to unravel the layers of inequality, challenge systemic biases, and foster an environment where economic opportunity is not a privilege but a human right.

In this endeavor, historical insights are a compass that guides us toward impactful change. They enable us to grasp the underlying currents that have shaped poverty's trajectory and chart a course that transforms lives meaningfully. A profound comprehension of the interplay between social and political forces can pave the way for interventions that create lasting change—interventions that address root causes and dismantle the very scaffolding that upholds the cycle of poverty.

At this juncture, let us remember that the struggle against poverty is a battle of ideologies, a contest between the status quo and the pursuit of equity. Let us honor the lessons etched in the annals of history, recognizing that the quest for a poverty-free world is not merely a policy agenda; it's a pledge to weave a new narrative, one where social and political influences converge to create a tapestry of opportunity, resilience, and dignity for all.

Economic Drivers of Poverty

The enduring grip of poverty across time finds its roots entangled with intricate economic variables. These threads, woven into the fabric of history, shed light on the tenacious nature of impoverishment. In eras preceding industrialization, the scarcity of pivotal resources, such as land and capital, cast a shadow over wealth accumulation prospects, thereby perpetuating poverty. An unbalanced distribution of these assets laid the foundation for a cycle of deprivation, impeding any substantial advancement.

Industrial Revolution's Paradox

The epochal advent of the Industrial Revolution ushered in an era of unprecedented transformation characterized by sweeping technological advancements that propelled societies into new dimensions of economic growth and development. This era bore the promise of unshackling humanity from the constraints of manual labor and subsistence existence, ushering in an age of boundless potential. However, the undercurrents of this monumental shift reveal a paradox that casts a long shadow upon its legacy.

Central to this paradox is the profound disjunction between the surge of progress and the glaring disparities in its distribution. Mechanization, driven by the ingenious minds of inventors and innovators, amplified industrial output to scales never before imagined. Factories roared to life, churning out goods with efficiency hitherto unfathomed. The surge in production unleashed the prospect of unparalleled prosperity as economies experienced unprecedented growth. Yet, beneath this cloak of progress, an insidious underbelly of inequality took root.

The principles of laissez-faire capitalism, lauded for their hands-off approach and belief in the self-regulating nature of markets, paradoxically laid the groundwork for a deeply stratified society. As capital flowed and industrial titans amassed fortunes, the benefits of this economic revolution were not shared equitably. The seeds of impoverishment were sown amidst the clamor of progress. While a privileged few reveled in opulence, the majority, comprising the toiling labor force that fueled the engines of industrialization, grappled with meager wages, wretched working conditions, and seemingly endless toil.

The machinery of progress, it seemed, turned a blind eye to the plight of the very individuals who drove its cogs. Workers, entrapped within this newly mechanized world, faced a disheartening reality. Their agency was curtailed, shackled by the power structures that had taken shape. The harsh reality of exploitation and dehumanizing labor practices offset the promise of liberation through technological marvels. The human toll was immense as generations endured arduous work hours, perilous conditions, and paltry compensation.

In retrospect, the paradox of the Industrial Revolution is not merely a historical footnote but a crucial chapter in understanding the dynamics of societal transformation. It illustrates the intricate interplay between progress and the imperative of equitable distribution. The lessons gleaned from this era resonate in modern times, serving as a poignant reminder that the unbridled march of progress, without conscious efforts to ensure parity, can inadvertently nurture the seeds of enduring inequality. As we navigate the complexities of technological advancement, this paradox remains a cautionary tale, a reminder that the true measure of progress lies not solely in economic output but in creating a society where prosperity flourishes universally.

The Dawning of Transformation: 20th Century's Complex Triumphs and Trials

The 20th century stands as a pivotal juncture in the annals of human history, where a symphony of intricate forces orchestrated a narrative of both triumphs and tribulations, reshaping the contours of poverty across the global stage. Technological marvels took center stage, unveiling the potency of innovation in steering economic metamorphosis.

Technological innovations ignited a blaze of efficiency as the century unfolded, illuminating new avenues for progress. The resulting economic expansion rippled across nations, rejuvenating dormant markets and kindling aspirations of prosperity. A profound promise surged for those relegated to the margins of income inequality. A vista of upward mobility emerged, casting hope upon the downtrodden.

Yet, this transformation was not a tale of unblemished advancement. The same mechanisms that propelled economic expansion also cast a long shadow of complexity. The narrative of uneven distribution unfolded, ushering in the stark duality of progress and inequality. While the beacon of economic upliftment shone bright, it cast enduring shadows of imparity. The tapestry of this era bore the intricate embroidery of triumphs interwoven with the threads of trials.

The 20th century's legacy reverberates through modern times, offering a mosaic of lessons. It is a testament to the capacity of human ingenuity to unravel new dimensions of growth. However, it serves as a poignant reminder that progress must be pursued with conscientious regard for the equitable distribution of its rewards. As we stride forward, these echoes guide us, urging us to embrace innovation while ensuring that the fruits of progress are woven into the fabric of society in a manner that banishes the specter of inequality and ushers in an era of shared prosperity.

Unraveling Contemporary Challenges

In the modern age, the landscape of poverty is intricately molded by the loom of global economic forces. This era is defined by the convergence of two influential currents: the sweeping tide of globalization and the rapid surge of automation. This juncture is marked by a profound reshaping of economic dynamics, bearing both opportunities and trials.

Globalization, the intricate interlinking of economies and cultures, takes center stage as a catalyst for change. Yet, this interwoven tapestry bears both threads of promise and challenges. The effects ripple across industries and nations as the world becomes increasingly interconnected. A surge in cross-border trade and investment bears the potential for economic growth but casts shadows over the stability of livelihoods. The interconnectedness that propels prosperity can sometimes serve as a conduit for disparities as shifts in production and market dynamics alter employment terrain.

At the forefront of this transformation stands the formidable force of rapid automation. Technological strides often hailed as heralds of progress, have cast a dual-edged sword. While unlocking new vistas of productivity and innovation, they simultaneously cast a shadow over traditional labor landscapes. Developed nations, often the harbingers of technological advancement, face the intricate dance of progress and displacement. Automation's relentless march, while revolutionizing industries, threatens conventional jobs, especially those that can be automated. The contours of poverty are thus reshaped as livelihoods hang in the balance.

In stark instances, diminished wages and the obliteration of jobs can emerge as unintended consequences of these global currents. The human toll can be profound as industries pivot and production landscapes shift. The very promise of interconnected prosperity can, paradoxically, magnify inequality. A conscious approach is imperative to navigate these challenges—a bridge between embracing innovation and mitigating its potential for disruption. In the unfolding story of globalization and automation, societies must craft strategies that empower workers, foster adaptable skill sets, and safeguard economic inclusion. Only through such vigilant endeavors can the shadows of poverty be gently unraveled from the intricate patterns woven by these global forces.

As we navigate this intricate journey of economic evolution, the necessity becomes apparent: comprehending the complex connections that link poverty and progress is the threshold to transformation. Governments are responsible for employing their legislative expertise in shaping a more equitable terrain. Formulating policies that ensure equitable access to resources, broaden the scope of job prospects, and gradually erode the foundation of inequality becomes paramount. Solely through such intentional and mindful endeavors can we aspire to unearth the root of persistent poverty and usher in an epoch where prosperity seamlessly intertwines with the very pattern of societal advancement.

Strategies for Individual Wealth Creation

Throughout the annals of history, humanity has ardently sought to transcend the clutches of poverty through a relentless pursuit of individual wealth creation. Many techniques have been deployed intricately shaped by the prevailing socio-political milieu. In eras preceding the Industrial Revolution, these strategies often hinged upon the intricate dance of access to land and accumulated wealth. A panoramic view reveals the interplay between personal aspiration and external constraints that have governed the evolution of wealth accumulation.

The pre-industrial epochs, fraught with limitations of resources and opportunities, witnessed the emergence of strategies tethered to societal frameworks. The spectrum of possibilities was dictated by one's social standing and proximity to power corridors. Landownership, often synonymous with economic security, stood as a primary conduit to wealth. However, the undercurrents of social hierarchies could render even this pathway inaccessible to the masses, further perpetuating the cycle of impoverishment.

The transformative Industrial Revolution introduced a paradigm shift, augmenting the toolkit for individual wealth ascent. Amidst the mechanized hum of progress, avenues emerged for those who could seize the opportunities unveiled. Enterprising individuals diversified their skills, invested in burgeoning enterprises, and charted entrepreneurial paths to affluence. Yet, it is paramount to recognize that these pathways were far from universal, as the dividends of industrialization remained confined within select echelons. The machinery of laissez-faire capitalism, while hailed for its potential to fuel economic prosperity, paradoxically sowed seeds of inequality, leaving swaths of the workforce mired in exploitative labor conditions.

In the 20th century, they revealed an intricate interplay of innovation and resourcefulness. The toolbox of wealth creation expanded, with novel techniques gaining prominence. The transformative power of education emerged as a potent instrument for enhancing earning potential, enabling individuals to transcend their circumstances by acquiring skills. Ventures into entrepreneurship, funded by judiciously saved funds or facilitated by accessible credit, sculpted new trajectories toward prosperity. These methods engineered success stories, emancipating some from the clutches of poverty. Yet, inherent within this narrative is the stark realization that the canvas of opportunities was not equally distributed as societal fissures persisted.

In the present epoch, individual wealth creation remains a beacon of hope in the battle against poverty. Governments endeavor to galvanize this pursuit through strategic policies, to offer tax incentives, to foster entrepreneurship, and to extend microfinance lifelines. However, despite these efforts, systemic barriers and gaps in comprehension often impede the transformative potential of these initiatives, leaving the most vulnerable strata untouched.

A reflection upon the historical tapestry of poverty unveils the intricate interplay of societal, political, and economic currents perpetuating its existence. Recognizing these multifaceted dynamics is quintessential in our endeavor to forge an equitable future. Armed with a nuanced understanding of historical intricacies, collaborative action beckons as we design policies that foster just access to resources and emancipate individuals from the throes of poverty.

The history accentuates that the quest for personal wealth has eternally been the compass guiding individuals toward prosperity. These strategies have repeatedly demonstrated their capacity to unshackle people from the bonds of deprivation, catalyzing economic upliftment. However, the progress is complete with acknowledging the influences of social and political landscapes. Crafting a transformative future mandates the development of policies that transcend mere economic considerations. They must be imbued with the spirit of equitable resource distribution and opportunities. Only through these purposeful strides can we herald a substantial and enduring transformation—one where the tendrils of poverty are delicately unwoven and the landscape of society is painted with strokes of lasting change.

CHAPTER TWO

TAKING CONTROL OF FINANCES

Making ends meet can feel like a Herculean endeavor that calls for a GPS navigator and mapmaker of the highest caliber. We must assess our current situation and determine our desired future course. Each person is also responsible for determining the most efficient way to reach their destination without wasting time or money on unnecessary detours. Relax and inhale deeply. Put your hands on your hips and shrug your shoulders. A few simple actions are all that are required. It may take a decade or more to accomplish some objectives.

To some extent, yes! Taking charge of all the money issues that have been bothering us might also have an instant benefit in the form of much less stress. Nine out of ten respondents in a 2019 survey reported that getting their money in order was the most important factor in their happiness and self-confidence. This chapter is your entry ticket to the party.

Synthesizing the Elements of Successful Wealth Creation Strategies

Many people aim to make money, yet doing so can frequently seem like a challenging undertaking. Avoid being seduced by get-rich-quick schemes and possibilities that seem too good to be true because they could lead you down a dangerous path. Achieving this objective requires patience, perseverance, and discipline. The good thing about this is that anyone can build and maintain money over time by using certain ideas and tactics. Additionally, your odds of success are increased the earlier you begin using these. We've listed several important wealth-building guidelines below, including establishing goals and creating a strategy, investing in education and skills, managing debt, saving money, investing it, safeguarding your assets, comprehending the effects of taxes, and establishing a solid credit history. This chapter will examine these principles in more detail and consider how they might help you reach your financial objectives.

1. Make Some Cash

You should start earning money right away. Although it may seem simple, this stage is the most important for people just starting. You've probably seen graphs demonstrating how little sums of money saved consistently and allowed to compound over time can eventually develop into substantial sums. But those graphs need to address the fundamental question of how to start saving money in the first place. Money can be made in two primary ways: actively and passively. Earned money is earned from your job, whereas passive income comes from investments. You might only have passive income once you have enough money to invest. These inquiries may help you choose what you want to accomplish and where your earned income will come from if you are either starting a career or thinking about changing careers:

2. What interests you?

By engaging in work that you enjoy and find meaningful, you will perform better, develop a career that will last longer, and increase your chances of financial success. Research revealed that more than 90% of workers would exchange a portion of their lifetime earnings for a job with more significance.

What do you excel at? Consider your strengths and how you may use them to support yourself. What will be lucrative? Consider occupations that fit what you excel at and enjoy doing and will fulfill your financial goals. The yearly Occupational Outlook Handbook released by the U.S. is a reliable resource for many industries' wage data and growth forecasts.

Where are you going? Find out what qualifications you need regarding education, experience, and training to pursue your desired job alternatives. Information about this is also available in the Occupational Outlook Handbook. You may get started in the correct direction by considering these factors. Investing in your education and talents is a smart move if you want to increase your earning potential. Higher degrees, certifications unique to your sector, and training courses are all beneficial ways to increase your human capital.

3. Create A Plan And Establish Goals

What purpose will you give your wealth? Do you want to save money for your future—possibly an early retirement? Paying for your children's college tuition? Purchase a second home? Give away some of your money to charity. The first step in accumulating wealth is setting goals. You may plan to get there after you know what you want to accomplish. Establish your financial objectives first, such as retiring early, purchasing a property, or paying off debt. Be precise about how much money you need to make each goal happen and when you plan to do it. After deciding on your objectives, you must create a strategy for accomplishing them. Making a budget to help you save more money, boosting your income through education or professional progression, or purchasing investments that will increase in value over time are some examples of how to do this. Your strategy should be practical, adaptable, and long-term oriented. Review your progress frequently and adapt as necessary to stay on course.

Save Some Cash

If you spend all of the money you earn, you won't be able to develop wealth. Moreover, it is essential to prioritize saving an adequate amount of money above all else, particularly when you do not possess sufficient funds to address your immediate financial obligations (such as bills, rent, or a mortgage) or unexpected emergencies. Many experts advise having three to six months' worth of salary saved up in case such circumstances arise. Consider making the following decisions to save more money for growing your wealth:

For at least a month, keep a record of your spending. A compact, pocket-sized notepad could also work, but you might wish to utilize financial software. Keep a record of every purchase you make, no matter how tiny; you'd be shocked where your money goes. Trim the fat where you can. You should budget for both necessities and luxuries. We can all agree that these necessities must be met. Health insurance, car insurance (if you have one), and life insurance (if you have a family) should also be factored in. More money will be spent, but not on necessities.

Determine a sum to save. After calculating your monthly savings goal, do your best to stick to your budget. This is not to say that frugal or minimalist lifestyles are always required. If your savings targets are being met, treat yourself and make occasional purchases (in an appropriate amount). You'll have a better outlook and more motivation to keep going. Activate automatic saving. Having your company or bank set up an automatic transfer of a specific amount of each paycheck into a different savings or investing account is a simple way to save a specific amount each month.

Similarly, you can contribute to your employer's 401(k) or other retirement plan by having money automatically deducted from your pay. Financial advisors typically advise making a minimum contribution to qualify for your employer's full match. Find savings with a good return. Search for savings accounts with the greatest interest rates and fewest fees to maximize the return on your funds. If you have the financial means to lock away your money for several months or years, certificates of deposit (CDs) may be an excellent choice for your savings. Also, keep in mind that cost-cutting can only be done so far. If your costs are currently low, you should consider measures to enhance your revenue.

Invest

After you have successfully saved some money, the following step is to invest it so that it will continue to grow. Having savings is quite important, yet the interest rates offered by bank accounts are sometimes rather low, and your money runs the risk of having its purchase power eroded over time due to inflation. For new investors (or any investor, for that matter), diversification is probably the most crucial notion. To put it plainly, you should try to diversify your investment portfolio. That's because investments behave differently depending on the time of year. For instance, bonds may be offering strong returns if the stock market is experiencing a losing stretch. Or, if Stock A is struggling, Stock B can be tearing it up. Due to their wide variety of investments in securities, mutual funds offer some built-in diversification. Additionally, investing in both a stock fund and a bond fund (or many stock funds and multiple bond funds, for example) instead of just one of each will result in better diversification.

Another generalization is that you can afford to take more risks when you're younger since you'll have more time to compensate for any losses. Investments come with different degrees of risk and possible return. The more secure an investment is, the lower the potential returns it typically offers, and vice versa. If you are not already aware of the many types of investments, you should learn about them through reading. Despite the vast selection of unusual investments that are accessible, the vast majority of investors will opt to begin their investment careers with traditional financial instruments such as bonds, equities, and mutual funds. Stocks are the tangible representation of a person's ownership stake in their company. Upon purchasing a company's stock, you assume the role of a partial shareholder, granting you rights to potential dividends or enhancements in the stock's value, as offered by the company. While it is widely understood that bonds generally carry a lesser risk than stocks, it's important to note that the associated hazards linked with stock investments can greatly fluctuate from one company to another.

Bonds serve a purpose analogous to that of IOUs issued by governments or corporations. When you buy a bond, the issuer guarantees they will return your initial investment plus interest at some point. Most people believe that bonds carry less risk than stocks but have less potential for appreciation. Credit rating agencies assign letter grades to bonds to indicate the varying levels of risk associated with different bonds. This practice acknowledges that certain bonds pose higher risks than others. Mutual funds, on the other hand, represent consolidated funds invested in a range of financial instruments, primarily including stocks, bonds, or a blend of both. By purchasing some shares in a mutual fund, you gain access to the fund as a whole. The level of risk that mutual funds pose might also change based on the investments that the funds choose to make.

Additionally, exchange-traded funds (ETFs) are similar to mutual funds in that each share contains the entirety of a portfolio of securities. However, ETFs are listed on exchanges and are traded similarly to stocks. Some ETFs follow specific industry sectors, asset classes like bonds and real estate, or important stock indices like the S&P 500.

Safeguard Your Assets

You put much effort into earning money and building your fortune. The worst-case scenario might be to lose everything due to an unexpected tragedy. Your home could be destroyed by fire, you could incur damage and medical costs from a car accident, or you could lose out on future income due to an early death. Insurance is essential to accumulating wealth because it offers protection from these and other dangers. In a fire, home insurance will rebuild your house and possessions, auto insurance will make you whole after a collision, and life insurance will pay your dependents in the event of an early death. Another sort of policy that will replace your income if you get hurt, sick, or otherwise incapacitated and unable to work is long-term disability insurance. Since insurance policies tend to cost more as you age, even young, healthy people should consider buying them. This means that purchasing life insurance now, even if you are 25 years old and unmarried, may be significantly more affordable than waiting until you are 30 and have a partner, kids, and a mortgage.

Reduce the Effects of Taxes

Taxes can hinder your efforts to accumulate wealth and are frequently disregarded. Of course, as we earn and spend money, we are all subject to income and sales taxes, but our investments and assets may also be subject to taxation. Understanding your tax vulnerabilities and creating plans to lessen their effects is crucial. Investing in tax-advantaged accounts is a simple approach to reducing your tax obligation. These accounts, including 401(k) plans, IRAs, and 529 college savings plans, have tax advantages that can increase your savings and lower your tax obligation. For instance, a typical IRA or 401(k) contribution allows you to lower your taxable income and save on taxes in the year you contribute. Additionally, because they grow tax-deferred, the effect will be less noticeable when you retire, and you are more likely to be in a lower tax rate. You can grow and withdraw money from a Roth account without paying taxes on any income or profits since investment earnings in a Roth IRA or 401(k) are tax-exempt.

Being careful with the time and location of your investments is another way to reduce taxes. By keeping investments for more than a year, you can benefit from the reduced long-term capital gains tax rate, typically lower than the short-term capital gains tax and income tax rates. Also, keep in mind the locations of various assets. If given the option, a tax-advantaged account like a Roth IRA should be used to hold an income-producing asset like a dividend-paying stock or corporate bond because these payments won't result in taxable events there. An investment in a growth stock that will solely result in capital gains (rather than income) may be more advantageously held in a taxable account.

Control Your Debt and Improve Your Credit

As your wealth increases, you'll see the value in taking on debt to finance different investments or purchases. Use a credit card to make purchases to get points or incentives. Exploring various possibilities, you can opt for a mortgage, a home equity loan tailored for house improvements, or an auto loan for purchasing a car. Alternatively, you might find yourself in a situation where a personal loan is necessary to kickstart your business venture or contribute to someone else's investment endeavor. However, handling your debt responsibly is crucial because accruing too much debt could impair your efforts to accumulate money. Pay attention to your debt-to-income (DTI) ratio when managing your debt, and make sure that your monthly debt payments fit comfortably into your spending plan. In order to avoid excessive interest charges, it's advisable to promptly settle high-interest debts, such as credit card balances. Exercise caution when dealing with products that involve variable or adjustable interest rates, like adjustable-rate mortgages (ARMs) or those involving balloon payments. Unforeseen shifts in the economy or your circumstances could potentially render these obligations unmanageable at a sudden notice. If you go into debt, it might hurt your credit score, and if you don't pay your debts, you could file for bankruptcy.

Keeping a High Credit Score

Long-term wealth growth and preservation depend heavily on establishing and keeping a high credit score. Suppose you have a solid credit history and a high credit score. Under such circumstances, you will experience advantages such as reduced interest rates and improved loan terms, leading to substantial savings amounting to thousands of dollars in interest payments over time.

Here are some essential actions you may take to keep a high credit score:

Punctually pay your expenses. Your payment history is a key element in determining your credit score. You must always pay your payments on time to keep your credit score high. Even a few days of late payments can significantly negatively affect your credit score.

Maintain minimal credit utilization. Another significant aspect that influences your credit score is your credit usage or how much of your available credit you utilize. You should keep your credit use below 30% of your available credit to retain a high credit score.

Keep an eye on your credit report. Checking your credit report frequently is a smart practice to ensure that all the data is accurate and current. Many services available today will provide you with a free credit report. Challenging any mistakes you notice on your credit report is critical because they might negatively influence your credit score.

Try to create only a few new accounts. Your credit score may be somewhat lowered each time you apply for credit. Only create a few new accounts quickly to keep your credit score high. However, remember that you risk having an insufficient credit history if you don't use credit cards or need adequate credit lines open. Open a few credit cards and obtain a few loans, but stay moderate.

You may maintain a decent credit score and increase your borrowing power over time by adhering to these guidelines and developing excellent credit habits.

Should I invest or pay off debt?

It normally makes sense to pay off high-interest debt before making investments if you have any, such as numerous credit card balances. Few investments ever yield returns as high as credit card fees. After successfully clearing your debt, redirect the surplus funds towards savings and investment opportunities. Whenever possible, make an effort to completely settle the full credit card balance each month to avoid accumulating interest charges.

How much cash is required to purchase a mutual fund?

Varied mutual fund providers have different entry-level investment minimums, frequently starting at around $500. You can typically invest less after that. Some mutual funds can waive their initial minimums provided you agree to make a consistent monthly investment. Via a brokerage firm, you also have the option to acquire shares in mutual funds and exchange-traded funds (ETFs). Some brokerage firms even offer the benefit of opening an account without any associated fees.

An exchange-traded fund (ETF) is what?

Similar to mutual funds, exchange-traded funds (ETFs) are investment pools. One significant distinction is that they trade their shares on stock exchanges (rather than buying and selling through a particular fund company). They occasionally impose lesser fees as well. You can also purchase them through a brokerage company with equities and bonds. While the allure of rapid wealth-building schemes can be tempting, the most reliable approach to amassing wealth remains consistent saving and investing, coupled with the patience to allow your money to flourish over time. Commencing with modest amounts is acceptable, yet initiating this process early on and maintaining a consistent effort is of utmost importance. Earn money, save it, and then wisely invest it. Insurance can help you safeguard your assets while reducing your tax liability. Remember that accumulating wealth is a process rather than a final goal. Along the road, celebrate your accomplishments and resist the urge to give up because of setbacks or difficulties. You can succeed financially and accumulate wealth over time if you have patience, discipline, and a clear understanding of your objectives.

Sustaining Momentum for Long-Term Impact

Different people define financial freedom differently. For many people, this entails having enough money to support their desired standard of living and having extra for retirement or to pursue any vocation without concern over pay. And isn't that what most of us aim to achieve when investing? But regrettably, too many people are hindered by debt and unexpected expenses, which keeps them from attaining their objectives. Furthermore, major disasters like earthquakes, hurricanes, and pandemics can highlight more gaps in safety nets. Make a plan and follow it to achieve all of your financial objectives, large and small, financial and lifestyle.

Make a budget for your finances that covers all of your living costs, and stick to it.

Pay off credit cards, monitor your credit score, and take on as little debt as possible.

Initiate the process of investing funds today with an eye on the future. The remarkable impact of compounding will lead to exponential growth of your money, though it's essential to allow sufficient time for substantial gains. While bear markets might discourage investors, it's important to recognize that profit opportunities still exist within such conditions.

Keep an eye on your spending. Make small changes that can greatly influence your financial health when distinguishing between what you want and need. You can create automated savings by setting up an emergency fund and paying for your employer's retirement plan. Your health should come first, even though maintaining your assets is less expensive than replacing them.

How Can We Achieve Financial Freedom More Quickly?

Start by considering the conventional investment options: sectoral funds, gold, debt funds, passive equity funds, and funds for debt. Each choice holds the potential for compounding, effectively doubling your assets over a decade. However, to achieve early financial independence, it's imperative to accelerate asset growth. This is where Wright Research's factor strategies come into play.

Factor strategies have the potential to yield unique returns beyond the conventional market standards by leveraging enduring market anomalies that have shown consistent success over extended periods. Customizing your investment approach through strategies such as Momentum, suitable for high-risk investors, or a Balanced Multi-Factor approach, preferable for those seeking a medium-risk profile, can substantially drive you closer to achieving your long-term financial goals.

Many people strive to reach the point of financial independence, defined as having sufficient savings, assets, and cash on hand to support one's preferred standard of living. Also, you should save enough money to retire comfortably or start a new job without feeling pressured to make a set amount every year. Sadly, far too many people never reach their financial goals. The growing debt they've accumulated due to frivolous spending is a persistent burden that prevents them from achieving their goals, even when unexpected costs are eliminated. The fragility of safety nets is highlighted when they are entirely overwhelmed by a catastrophic event. Almost anyone has bad times, but if you adopt these behaviors, you'll be well on your way to overcoming adversity.

Prioritize Your Life

Financial independence is a shared aspiration, yet its pursuit demands a clearer definition. While the desire is universal, it's essential to establish precise objectives in terms of amounts and timelines. To enhance your likelihood of success, ensure that your goals are as explicit as possible.

Here are three things to aim for:

- What a reasonable amount of money would be to do that
- When must that sum be saved, and by what age?
- The necessities of your way of existence

Then, from your target age backward to your actual age, set monetary milestones between the two ages at appropriate times. Put the target sheet at the beginning of your budget binder, and write down all the amounts and due dates.

Create a Monthly Budget

Establishing and consistently following a monthly household budget is the most dependable approach to guaranteeing the coverage of all expenditures and the achievement of savings targets. This practice becomes a valuable habit that maintains your concentration on objectives and aids in resisting the impulse to indulge in unnecessary expenses.

Repaying Credit Card Debt in Full

Debt from credit cards and other high-interest consumer loans is detrimental to financial success. Always pay the full balance at the end of the month. Interest rates for student loans, mortgages, and similar loans are substantially lower, so eliminating them is not an immediate financial crisis.

Making on-time payments on these loans is still crucial despite their lower interest rates.

Make a Plan for Regular Savings

Invest in your financial security first. Take advantage of your company's matching contribution benefit by enrolling in their retirement plan. It's also a good idea to set up a recurring deposit into a brokerage account or something similar and a withdrawal to an emergency fund that can be used for unforeseen costs. Money for savings accounts like an emergency fund and retirement plan should be automatically deducted from your salary the day it is deposited. Remember that the money you should set aside in an emergency fund depends on your situation. You shouldn't rely only on a tax-advantaged retirement plan as an emergency fund because of the stringent withdrawal limits associated with such accounts.

Begin Making Investments Immediately

Although bear markets cause some to question the value of the investment, there has been no better method to build your money throughout history. If you give compound interest enough time, your money will grow exponentially, but only after a very long period. Nevertheless, remember that amateurs should refrain from trying to emulate the stock-picking success of billionaires like Warren Buffett. Instead, sign up for an online brokerage account that will help you learn about investing, build a portfolio you can handle, and automatically add to it every week or month. To get you started, we evaluated the top online brokers for newcomers.

Check Your Credit Report Regularly

A new vehicle loan or mortgage refinancing interest rate is directly proportional to a borrower's credit score. The cost of other necessities, such as auto and life insurance, is also affected. One's credit score has more weight because of the assumption that a person careless with their money is also likely to be careless with their health, their vehicle, or both.

This is why checking your credit report frequently is crucial to ensure no inaccurate negative entries. For further security, you should subscribe to a trustworthy credit monitoring service.

Concede a Price for Products and Services

People in the United States often avoid haggling because they worry it will make them look poor. You could save thousands of dollars annually if you can overcome your fear. Particularly with smaller firms, it pays to buy in bulk or establish yourself as a regular customer to get the best deals.

Never Stop Learning About Money Matters

Each year, you should check the tax code to ensure you take advantage of all the deductions and credits you can. Be bold and change your investment strategy based on what you learn by following the news and watching the stock market. As a bonus, being well-informed is your best defense against con artists that target inexperienced investors for financial gain.

Pay Attention to Repairs

Taking care of your belongings will extend the life of everything from your automobile and lawn mower to your shoes and wardrobe. Compared to the replacement price, maintenance is a wise investment.

Don't Spend More Than You Earn

It's easier than you might think to master a frugal lifestyle by training your mind to be content with less. Before becoming affluent, many successful people got into the practice of living frugally. The transition to minimalism is relatively easy. Small changes can tremendously impact your financial well-being, so learning to distinguish between needs and wants is important.

Be mindful of your physical well-being

Taking exceptional care of your body follows the principle of regular maintenance, which has a major positive effect on your financial health. It's simple to put money toward improved health. This involves making regular visits to healthcare professionals such as doctors or dentists and taking action based on their advice for any health concerns you might have. Modifying aspects like diet and exercise regimens can, for instance, enhance or even avert various health issues. But neglecting your health, directly and indirectly, impacts your ability to achieve your goals financially. Some firms don't provide any more when paid sick days are exhausted. Increased insurance costs due to obesity and other dietary-related disorders; early retirement due to poor health, with a resulting permanent reduction in monthly income.

Defining Your Place on the Path to Financial Freedom

Financial independence takes on many personal forms, varying with each individual's unique aspirations. It emerges as a diverse embodiment, reflecting various dreams and goals. To many, it represents a substantial financial safety net – a fusion of savings, investments, and readily accessible funds – capable of sustaining a lifestyle free from economic constraints. The crux of this concept revolves around attaining a level of abundance that transcends the essentials. Whether earmarked for ensuring a secure retirement or fueling personal passions, the aim is to break free from the perpetual pull of financial stress.

This pursuit parallels sculpting a life where economic necessity no longer dictates decisions. Financial independence is a transformative force, enabling the unfettered pursuit of dreams and aspirations. It involves anchoring these ambitions in a solid fiscal framework that lends stability and empowerment. The spectrum of possibilities is broad and varied – from nurturing artistic endeavors to embarking on journeys around the globe. Ultimately, it's about crafting a life where prosperity serves as a conduit to holistic well-being, dispelling apprehensions about the future and allowing for an embrace of the present with open arms.

This journey toward financial freedom isn't solely a financial endeavor; it's a deeply personal and transformative voyage. It encapsulates the aspiration to engineer a life that isn't hindered by monetary worries. Achieving financial independence isn't just about accumulating wealth; it signifies a shift in mindset, a conscious choice to build a life that aligns with individual passions and aspirations. This isn't a one-size-fits-all journey; it's an exploration that resonates differently with each person. It's a reflection of the unique dreams that shape us as individuals.

For some, financial independence signifies the security of knowing that they have sufficient funds to cover their basic needs and unforeseen expenses. The tranquility stems from the assurance that unforeseen financial difficulties won't disrupt their plans. For some, it signifies the freedom to follow their enthusiasms and hobbies without being confined by a rigid budget. This could involve embarking on new experiences, exploring interests, or devoting time to charitable pursuits.

Moreover, the essence of financial independence lies not just in the present but also in the ability to plan for the future confidently. It means having the resources to retire comfortably and pursue experiences that might have seemed out of reach during the years of active work. It's the freedom to savor the golden years without the stress of financial instability.

The path to financial freedom demands careful planning, disciplined execution, and a profound understanding of one's financial landscape. It begins with setting clear financial goals, both short-term and long-term. Defining what financial independence means to you is pivotal – whether it's retiring at a certain age, owning a home, paying for your children's education, or launching your own business. These goals serve as the guiding compass for your financial choices and behaviors. Formulating a budget that resonates with your goals and principles is crucial to achieving financial autonomy. A budget isn't about restricting yourself; it's about channeling your resources toward what truly matters to you. It's a tool that empowers you to allocate funds intentionally, ensuring that your spending reflects your priorities. Thoroughly monitoring your expenses and income is paramount; it reveals patterns, accentuates opportunities for enhancement, and furnishes a comprehensive snapshot of your financial well-being.

In the pursuit of financial independence, saving becomes an invaluable ally. Cultivating a savings habit – consistently setting aside a portion of your income – is the cornerstone of building financial resilience. Emergency funds act as a lifeline in the face of unforeseen setbacks, offering protection against the potential disruptions stemming from unexpected costs such as medical bills or home repairs. At the same time, directing funds toward retirement accounts constitutes a strategic move, cultivating lasting financial stability.

Investment represents another critical facet of this journey. It entails safeguarding wealth and facilitating the expansion of your funds over time. Achieving diversity in your investment portfolio across various asset classes minimizes risk and maximizes potential opportunities. Understanding your risk tolerance is vital; it ensures your investment choices align with your comfort level and long-term goals.

However, the path to financial independence is open to challenges. It requires discipline, adaptability, and an unwavering commitment to your goals. Economic shifts, personal setbacks, and unexpected expenses might temporarily alter your trajectory. Yet, the essence lies in resilience – the ability to recalibrate, learn from setbacks, and stay the course.

In this journey, seeking knowledge and advice is a sign of wisdom. Educating yourself about personal finance, investment strategies, and retirement planning empowers you to make informed decisions. Consulting financial advisors can provide valuable insights tailored to your specific circumstances. They help align your financial approach with your aspirations, ensuring that every step you take is purposeful and informed.

Pursuing financial independence is a symphony of intention, action, and mindset. It's about crafting a life where financial worries no longer wield control and dreams are pursued without hesitation. It embodies a well-balanced existence, where financial stability isn't an end but a means to savoring life's journey. As you carve your unique path toward financial freedom, remember that each step, no matter how small, is a stride toward transforming aspirations into reality.

Demystifying the 50/30/20 Budget Rule

The ingenious 50/30/20 budget rule, championed by Senator Elizabeth Warren, serves as a compass to steer individuals toward fiscal equilibrium. The formula proposes a judicious allocation of after-tax income:

- Dedicate half, a pragmatic 50%, to cover essential needs.
- Allot 30% for discretionary desires that enrich life's tapestry.
- Reserve the remaining 20% for a twin focus on savings and easing the debt burden.

This rule transcends mere numbers; it's a voyage into the heart of financial prudence. Embracing the 50/30/20 rule catalyzes budgetary alignment and instills mindfulness about expenditure priorities. Envision it as a roadmap to cultivate healthy financial habits, leading to fiscal autonomy's pinnacle. To empower this journey, we offer a streamlined tool - a compass to navigate your financial landscape, fostering the transformation from fiscal chaos to a symphony of financial independence.

Navigating the Interplay of Credit Scores and Auto Insurance Premiums

The intricate connection between credit scores and auto insurance rates paints a fascinating canvas of financial dynamics. While numerous jurisdictions restrict or prohibit credit scores for such evaluations, many insurance companies still employ credit-based scoring systems to assess coverage eligibility and premium rates.

Delving deeper, this interplay underscores the multifaceted factors that insurers consider when gauging risk. A lower credit score, often reflecting financial challenges, might be perceived as an indicator of heightened risk, potentially leading to higher insurance premiums. On the other hand, those with more favorable credit scores might be deemed more financially stable and, therefore, eligible for more competitive rates.

Interestingly, certain states, including Hawaii, Washington, California, Massachusetts, and Michigan, take a distinctive stance, curbing the use of credit scores as a determinant in insurance pricing. These states champion a more equitable approach, recognizing that socio-economic variances shouldn't disproportionately impact one's access to affordable coverage.

The landscape unveils legislation's critical role in safeguarding fairness in insurance practices. As individuals, understanding the nuances of these regulations empowers us to advocate for a balanced and just evaluation of risk and cost. This intersection of credit scores and insurance premiums serves as a reminder that the path to financial equilibrium is intrinsically tied to the decisions we make, the policies that shape industries, and the quest for inclusivity on the road to financial security.

Shaping a Better, More Prosperous Future for All

In the relentless pursuit of progress, paramount imperative surfaces: enhancing the quality of life for every member of society. The envisioned future is one of thriving individuals, grounded in the understanding that a nation's prosperity is inseparably intertwined with the well-being of its people.

The core of forging a flourishing society rests on a fundamental principle: channeling resources into people. This principle demands dismantling barriers that impede anyone within the nation from pursuing their aspirations with conviction and dignity. Rejecting the notion that destitute individuals are condemned to perpetual poverty, the objective is to equip them for economic autonomy. Central to this mission is ensuring that each societal member is granted the chance to learn, progress, and positively influence their immediate circles.

Acknowledging that robust health, education, and workforce readiness propel success, it's evident that individuals are better positioned to meet their essential needs and attain prosperity when fortified with these core components. This ripple effect extends to their families and communities, exemplifying the crucial role of early education as a catalyst for future accomplishments. Investing in early learning programs lays the foundation for elevated achievements among citizens. Complementing this effort is a resilient and affordable childcare system that empowers workers to dedicate themselves to their careers, enhancing individual and collective triumph. The symbiotic relationship between thriving local enterprises and a resilient economy further underscores the lasting dividends of today's investments in top-tier childcare facilities.

Akin in significance to fostering economic independence is stable, reasonably priced housing availability. Beyond being a mere shelter, housing is the nucleus of family life—a haven for raising children, fostering connections with neighbors, and aging gracefully. Without secure housing, contributing meaningfully to society becomes an arduous task.

Additional conduits for investing in human capital and stimulating economic growth encompass youth engagement, advanced education, job creation, promoting active lifestyles, and cultivating secure neighborhoods. Governments worldwide shoulder the onus of directing resources toward social development initiatives that tangibly alleviate poverty. Recognizing the supreme value of human capital, it's imperative to explore avenues beyond government involvement to pursue uplifting investments. The mission to ensure universal prosperity and combat poverty necessitates the collaborative endeavors of diverse entities and institutions.

A Collective Imperative: Pioneering a Path to a Radiant Future

The progression of civilization pivots on the combined aptitude to cooperate, accumulate knowledge, and take resolute action. The steadfast dedication to shaping a fairer future rests on a fundamental principle: channeling resources into humanity's potential. This principle is the pivotal axis upon which the yearning for a more balanced society and the fight against poverty revolves.

This isn't just a concept; it's an empowering dynamic that propels the pursuit of a more impartial society. The journey toward this goal relies on the potential inherent in collective resource sharing and harmonious collaboration. This endeavor extends its nurturing grasp to educational avenues, laying the groundwork for the flowering of knowledge and potential. It widens career horizons, empowering individuals to contribute meaningfully to communities and society.

However, the momentum continues. Unified efforts also manifest in robust health and wellness initiatives, strengthening society's members' physical and mental resilience. Simultaneously, the assurance of housing security nurtures a sense of belonging, fostering connections and stability that reverberate beyond individual lives and intertwine with the very fabric of the community.

In this shared endeavor, the rewards of labor are reaped. Architects of progress emerge as creators of opportunity and advocate for a brighter future. The synergy of collaboration reverberates through generations, resonating with the spirit of unity, determination, and collective purpose. The shared commitment to investing in individuals and, in turn, elevating society unveils the pathway to a future that is not only brighter but also rich in prosperity, compassion, and boundless human potential.

Empowering Financial Autonomy Through People-Centric Investments

Unlocking the potential of a secure and prosperous future necessitates a determined stride toward financial autonomy. This journey is ignited by an unwavering dedication to extracting maximum value from every dollar, paving the way for an elevated life for oneself and cherished ones. At its core, this endeavor revolves around a fundamental principle: investing in the growth and development of individuals, a gesture that inherently amplifies the prospects of all. The dividends yielded by such investments reverberate across time, coalescing into an enduring legacy of progress and affluence.

The road to financial independence and abundance is charted through unyielding commitment and astute savings practices. The present juncture beckons as the opportune crossroads to embark on this expedition, leaving no room for any obstacle to hinder the journey. The blueprint for a secure financial future unfurls, compelling immediate action. Unified in our intent, we stand poised to reshape the contours of the horizon that stretches ahead.

This journey, though rooted in personal aspirations, is inherently communal. It echoes the collective yearning for self-reliance and prosperity, a desire reverberating through diverse individuals and families. As we synchronize our pursuits, we amplify the ripples of progress, creating a tapestry of financial empowerment that transcends the boundaries of the present moment. In financial autonomy, every stride we take towards prudent investments and diligent savings is a stride towards the empowerment of communities, bolstering collective well-being, and fortifying our shared future.

The capacity to forge a brighter, more prosperous future for everyone becomes resoundingly evident in unity. The clarion call to action reverberates channel resources toward aspirations, invest in people, and thus usher in an era of shared abundance. The odyssey toward this realization commences today, and as our endeavors harmonize, we witness aspirations materializing into tangible accomplishments. The unequivocal verity persists: investing in people perpetually reaps bountiful rewards.

Investing Wisely and Strategically

Investing is more than just a buzzword; it's an intelligent way to improve your financial situation, save for the future, and preserve your hard-earned wealth. However, to reap the benefits in the future, action must be taken right now. Anyone can be dug out of poverty by investing as early as possible. But where do we begin, exactly? When you reach that point, what do you do?

When do you invest?

To invest is to put money or other resources into something with the expectation of future financial gain. You can put your money, time, or energy into something.

Types of Investments that are Commonly Used:

- Stock exchanges
- Money Market Funds (ETFs)
- Equity
- Cryptocurrency
- Homeownership

We'll go into the nitty-gritty of these five common investment strategies briefly.

What is the process of investing?

Money can be made through investments, but they are also a form of gambling. The adage says, "You need to spend money to make money." Money spent in a business, for instance, can be used to expand the firm's operations and, with any luck, boost income. Therefore, the company and its stocks should increase in value. That's how you, the investor, benefit as well.

Gains can be reaped from investments in two ways:

Interest payments received from bonds and dividends gained from stocks are recurring disbursements provided to investors as a gesture of appreciation or motivation. A dividend is essentially an allotment of a company's profits to its shareholders, usually presented as a predetermined percentage of those earnings (e.g., $1 per share if the share price is $30). The item or product you purchased increased in value over time, allowing you to sell it for more than you paid for it. This occurs because people see the worth in what you've built (partly because of the sizable dividends or interest payments).

After that, they're interested in buying some shares, increasing the price. You would have made a nice profit if you bought shares at $5 each and sold them at $25. Investing in real estate properties follows a similar logic, albeit with some subtle differences: If you rent out your investment property, you can count on a steady monthly income. If the home appreciates over time, you could see a greater return on investment. Whether you're buying stocks, bonds, bitcoin, or a house, investing only makes sense if the value of your investment rises over time.

Why Should One Put Money Into Investment?

The primary advantage of investing is financial gain (and without any extensive labor, to boot). The paycheck is important, but there's more to it than that. You can benefit from investing by:

Fight price increases and the dollar's declining purchasing power annually with inflation protection. The money you have right now is well-spent if you put it to good use. Maintaining purchasing power requires that your savings increase at a rate at least as fast as inflation.

You should start saving and investing as soon as possible to be financially secure in retirement. Putting money aside now will allow your investments plenty of time to grow in value and accrue interest (interest on your interest). With strategic planning, it's conceivable to retire and sustain yourself using the earnings from your investments. By making use of tax-deferred retirement plans such as a 401(k) or an Individual Retirement Account (IRA), you have the option to delay the payment of taxes on the money you add to these accounts until the point at which you opt to take them out in your years of retirement. Instead, taxation will occur during the withdrawal process.

Most persons are at a higher tax rate when making deposits than when making withdrawals, which means they may be able to reduce their income tax liability by doing so. You should invest your money and leave it invested if you have a spending problem—the opportunity to save money and curb the desire to spend increases. Keep and grow your wealth over time since smart investing can free you from living paycheck to paycheck. Saving more money may be possible if you commit to making small, incremental payments to create future wealth. As a result, you'll be able to reinvest more money and experience a much more positive cycle.

How Much Of A Profit Can You Expect To Make?

- Your portfolio's risk level will determine your expected rate of return (ROI):
- Low-risk equities and government bonds are examples of reasonably secure investments.
- Over the previous one hundred years, it has ranged from 6.1 % to 7.7 %.
- The average return on a diversified portfolio is 8.7 percent.
- Annualized returns of 9.4% to 10.3% have been typical for high-risk investments (often called a "growth portfolio").

Despite these overarching statements, everything is relative. Unless the return on investment has decreased from the previous three years (when it was at 9%, 10%, and 11%), an ROI of 7% is considered quite good for an individual investment.

Investing Entails Some Risk, Right?

There's a constant potential for partial or complete loss of invested funds. Nonetheless, tactics exist to mitigate the overall risk of investments: Allocate your funds to secure options such as CDs, government bonds, and dividend stocks. Diversify your investments across multiple avenues. Your portfolio should still generate a healthy return, even if some individual stocks or bonds decline.

Keep your money invested through periods of uncertainty; following a dip, the value of most low- to medium-risk investments eventually recovers. If you cash out your shares when they are at a low price, you are locking in a loss. Get cheap, then sell high. There's a good reason why this investment maxim has stood the test of time. When the market is down, it's a good time to buy shares since there's nowhere for their value to go but up if you invest sensibly.

Where Should I Start With Investing?

You've taken the first step in the right direction by reading this far. There are several things that every first-time investor should do regardless of whether they want to invest in stocks, ETFs, or cryptocurrency. Make a plan to save money that considers your actual financial situation. Saving up enough money to invest without choosing between paying rent and purchasing food is the first step. Although experts advise putting away 20% of your paycheck each month, most young folks would be better off setting aside 10%. Your salary and other debts, such as student loans, should go toward this aim as much as possible. Determine your investment objectives by figuring out what you hope to achieve financially. Maintaining a regular interest income may require selecting low-risk investments and steady long-term growth possibilities. At the same time, investors seeking higher returns may prefer investments with greater potential for both.

Some consumers may prefer to invest through a mobile app without first talking to a financial advisor. However, a financial advisor can help you make selections that align with your goals and even manage your portfolio on your behalf if you're serious about growing your wealth through prudent investment decisions.

Putting Money Into Stocks

Stocks are an excellent place to begin because of the breadth of options available, from low-risk to high-risk investments in practically any industry, with the potential for immediate and long-term gains. Learn the basics of stock investing here:

Get started by opening an account; you can buy stocks with or without the assistance of a financial advisor, depending on the type of account you choose. Pick the right bank account for you: Trading stocks and other investments through a brokerage account. Consider the broker's fees, investment choices, and reputation before signing up with them. You can use them to open a tax-deferred or tax-paying account and start investing. A robo-advisor account is similar to an individual retirement account (IRA) investing on your behalf in the stock market. Your portfolio will be managed for a nominal cost. Another low-maintenance choice is an employer-sponsored 401(k) plan, in which you can buy shares of stock through a mutual fund but typically not directly. Long-term success can be expected from this hands-off strategy.

Make a plan for your money — experts agree that stock market investments should account for a very small percentage of a diversified portfolio. They recommend allocating the remaining funds to stock and bond mutual funds, which are less risky and more conducive to long-term savings. Spend time analyzing your account statements once a quarter to examine the growth of each stock or fund in your portfolio. Put greater weight on long-term growth than short-term volatility, as the latter obscures the more meaningful underlying patterns. Many of these crucial measures also apply to other asset categories.

Putting Money Into A Mutual Fund

Again, opening an account is the first step toward making money through mutual funds. Your options for investing in your child's future post-secondary education are similar to those for stock investment: You can open an Individual Retirement Account (IRA), a Company Retirement Plan (401(k), or a brokerage account), or an Education Savings Account (ESA).

Following that, think about the following:

Invest in mutual funds; nevertheless, many have high entry requirements. For example, Vanguard is, so you'll need to set aside enough money to reach the minimum before investing in the fund of your choice. Remember that mutual fund transactions can only be made once each day, at the closure of the stock market. One advantage of mutual funds is that investors are not limited to making purchases in multiples of the share price. Like stocks, you need to keep tabs on your asset growth and adjust as needed. Setting up automatic installments will help you steadily amass wealth over time.

Purchasing Exchange Traded Funds

Exchange-traded funds are similar to equities and mutual funds in several ways: They can be bought and sold on stock exchanges like stocks at any time of the day with no minimum investment. They share characteristics with mutual funds in that they are constructed from a wide range of assets. You can start investing when you open an account with a brokerage or a robo-advisor. If you're handling your brokerage account management, consider the following criteria when choosing which ETFs to invest in:

The cost ratio quantifies the degree to which administrative expenses affect your overall profits. Unlike active ETFs, passive ETFs aim to replicate the outcomes of a market index, such as the S&P 500, rather than actively trading individual stocks. Conversely, actively managed exchange-traded funds (ETFs) offer investors an opportunity to outperform the index by taking advantage of short-term price fluctuations. The popularity of an ETF is gauged by the volume of its shares bought and sold during a specified period, but not necessarily by its performance. While past results do not guarantee future success, they do provide insight into the potential for sustained growth (or lack thereof). The bid/ask spread refers to the difference between the buying and selling prices of an ETF.

The term "bid" describes the highest purchase price offered for a security or investment vehicle. The asking price is the minimum value a seller is willing to part with their stock. The gap between these figures encompasses the entire cost of a complete round-trip transaction. This constitutes a potential loss if you buy and sell this fund in the future. The bid/ask spread holds greater significance when engaging in active ETF trading.

Putting Your Money Into Crypto

Buying cryptocurrency is similar to investing in stocks or exchange-traded funds (ETFs), except that rather than buying shares in a company, you are purchasing a digital currency whose worth is tied to the value of the currency as a whole. This is a guide on how to put your money into Bitcoin. To buy or sell cryptocurrency, you must use an exchange. Typically, this takes the form of an app that lets you exchange your dollars for another currency. The initial stage of purchasing cryptocurrency involves selecting the specific cryptocurrency you intend to buy (Bitcoin being the most recognizable, although Ethereum, Litecoin, and others are also accessible) and determining the quantity of coins (or portions of coins) you wish to acquire. Store it in your "wallet" — a digital wallet is a software application or hardware tool designed for storing and facilitating cryptocurrency transactions (commonly through an exchange).

Putting Money Into Property

Since most physical property increases in value over time, any purchase might be considered an investment in real estate. You can, however, enter the real estate investment market via a plethora of alternative routes, both active and passive: Professionally managed trusts known as Real Estate Investment Trusts (REITs) employ investor capital to acquire, operate, rent out, and sell real estate, with the proceeds being distributed to the trust's shareholders. Like other forms of passive investment, real estate mutual funds allow you to profit from the real estate market without being involved in purchasing and selling individual properties.

Real estate managers or companies form Real Estate Limited Partnerships (RELPs) to fund massive projects like shopping malls or five-star resorts. These types of passive investing possibilities carry a higher level of risk than certain others but can pay off handsomely in the end. Those who want to invest in real estate but need more knowledge might look at pre-vetted rental homes. Properties that have already been prepared for renters are an alternative. It's riskier than picking individual properties but less passive than investing in a fund or trust. Investors are especially active in purchasing properties that need work. However, you get to make all the decisions regarding the house, the renovation, and the selling. Buying a home needing repair and turning it into a rental or flipping it for a profit is a high-risk strategy.

Many experts in the field of finance propose that novice investors construct diversified portfolios consisting of low- to medium-risk assets with the potential for long-term growth. It's likely that your 401(k), individual retirement accounts (IRA), or Roth IRA will have earned a considerable return by the time you retire and start taking money. Investing in stocks and funds managed by a robo-advisor can help you get your feet wet in the market and learn the ropes so that you can eventually support on your own. Low-risk investment options include exchange-traded funds (ETFs) and index funds, which both follow a market index. Many have no minimum investment requirement and cheap fees, making them ideal for novices with limited funds. Investments should be made at any age (or at least thinking about investing). That way, you can save for the long haul and the smaller expenses that crop up along the road.

CHAPTER THREE
PURSUING ENTREPRENEURSHIP AND SMALL BUSINESS VENTURES

Creating jobs through entrepreneurship allows parents in low-income neighborhoods to provide clothing for their children. Employment permits community members to give healthcare all year round instead of short-term healthcare programs that provide healthcare for a few months. Farmers and other "own-account" employees comprise most developing nations' labor force. "Small-scale entrepreneurs" are likelier to be poor because of their business models.

In order to help the working poor find a way out of poverty, it is crucial to give self-employed people the tools they need to increase their job and income security. Entrepreneurship that generates employment is an excellent method to help the poor lift themselves out of poverty. There is widespread agreement that alleviating poverty in rural regions should be a priority for international development efforts, yet conventional approaches have limitations.

With its creative approach to social issues, social entrepreneurship is emerging as a promising new strategy for addressing rural poverty through sustainable development. Finding, creating, and acting upon social opportunities are what social entrepreneurs do. Social, economic, and ecological deprivation each contribute to the unique social opportunities in rural areas. Incorporating farmers into their value chain to create and realize social potential is a long-term solution to poverty.

Businesses may suffer when people are living in poverty. Illiteracy is a common factor in low-income situations and has been shown to reduce output. Workers with limited literacy may need help following procedures. As a result, they are more likely to make mistakes on the job, leading to financial losses and a drop in patron confidence. Businesses may suffer when people are living in poverty. Having a lower level of education is correlated with living in poverty.

Workflow instructions can be challenging to interpret for employees with low literacy levels. As a result, they are more likely to make mistakes on the job, leading to financial losses and a drop in patron confidence. Businesses may also feel the effects of poverty in their surrounding community. Due to financial instability, some people may resort to criminal behavior to make ends meet. The cycle of poverty and crime is only reinforced when businesses leave a neighborhood with high crime rates because it is no longer a viable place to operate. To break this vicious cycle, businesses should work to reduce poverty rather than exacerbate it. Small businesses have the potential to make a positive difference in their communities, and thriving neighborhoods are good for business.

The inability to get necessary goods and services is a major contributor to poverty. Businesses may help by giving low-income individuals and communities access to training and funding opportunities. Citizens who have received skill training can better compete for high-paying employment. Poor communities can use financing to establish cooperatives and businesses to help them escape poverty. For instance, people who want to create their businesses may apply for microloans from financial institutions like banks. If they have collateral, consistent income, or a credit history that can be verified, they may be able to get a loan from a traditional bank. As a result, they may have to resort to borrowing money at exorbitant interest rates, effectively cutting into their disposable income.

Conversely, microloans are short-term loans of a modest amount that have more lenient payback terms. Poor business owners can increase their income with the help of microloans without jeopardizing their ability to repay their debt. Businesses can further aid in the fight against poverty by creating economic opportunities for women. Women can become financially independent of their husbands if they are taught how to start and run their businesses. If their spouses become disabled, women can still provide for their families, and their children will not have to adjust to a lower standard of living. Putting money into empowering women is a smart business move. Women's access to economic resources improves their families' health, education, and economic security, which in turn creates a more robust and productive labor force and consumer base.

Public health concerns are exacerbated by insufficient water supply and poor sanitation. Water-borne diseases, including diarrhea, hepatitis, and cholera, can spread when individuals don't have access to safe drinking water. Poor sanitation can lead to health problems like parasite infections in the gut. Illnesses like these might cause workers to miss time from work and reduce output.

Businesses of varying sizes have the opportunity to contribute to the battle against water scarcity and inadequate sanitation by aiding in the establishment of public water systems and the development of personal sanitation infrastructure. Ensuring sufficient water availability and secure sanitation will lead to improved well-being and higher efficiency among employees, as well as the proper functioning of business establishments, given the essential role water plays in maintaining these commercial facilities. Businesses may help those in need by funding initiatives that boost infrastructure and services in disadvantaged areas. Consumers are better positioned to take advantage of firms' wares and services when living conditions improve. When companies do well, so does the whole neighborhood.

How to Manage a Small Business

"Small business management" describes coordinating and harmonizing a small company's many moving parts, such as its personnel, suppliers, financial resources, strategic direction, and day-to-day operations. The proprietor of a small business needs special help carrying out daily operations. Aside from the fundamentals of running a small business, you'll need expertise in accounting, H.R., and the relevant laws and regulations.

In most cases, the SBA considers a company small if it has less than 500 employees. The government often assists small enterprises. The United States Census Bureau estimates that 99.7 percent of all enterprises in the country are considered to be small. The SBA considers other metrics besides employee count when deciding who qualifies as a small business. Some questions to ask about a company include whether or not it is American-based and run, whether or not it is majority or minority-owned, whether or not it is profitable, and so on.

Businesses fall into the "small business" category because their managerial and operational difficulties differ greatly from giant organizations. Companies can qualify for government contracts and receive funding for expansion if they consider themselves small businesses. A company can also have access to resources that can help it compete with larger firms. In contrast to multinational conglomerates, small firms often operate on smaller budgets and with less bureaucracy, and they may only serve a limited geographic area. High-quality customer service and innovative problem-solving are common priorities for these businesses. Management of a small corporation encompasses every facet of operations, from finances and human resources to marketing and new product development.

The Importance of Small Business Management

As any business owner will tell you, good management is the key to keeping your company afloat over the long haul. Managing a small business presents special obstacles that need to be addressed when dealing with a larger organization. When it comes to commercial matters, for instance, business owners and leaders can benefit greatly from the perspective offered by small business management. It especially accounts for the fact that small business owners are more likely to have one-on-one interactions with their staff, requiring them to have excellent people skills and the ability to think on their feet.

Another advantage of adopting a small business attitude is the ability to save time and automate repetitive processes that divert you from your business goals. The time and money you save by looking for ways to cut corners might add up to a significant sum. A small business mindset recognizes the importance of this distinction from the management guidance offered to giant organizations.

How Can You Develop The Necessary Abilities To Run A Small Business Successfully?

The management of small businesses calls for one's whole attention and a special set of abilities. While tenacity, resolve, and exertion are essential, so is the ability to spot opportunities to speed up the process. Just think of what you could accomplish in an extra 15 minutes every day. Saving even a few minutes a day adds up to many days by the end of the year. Thoughtful, long-term planning is just as important as time and effort. With the Fresh Books product suite, you can reclaim lost time and streamline business operations to boost productivity and profitability.

Management of a small business entails coordinating all aspects of the company to ensure its continued growth and success, including but not limited to the creation of the business, the determination of funding requirements, the management of employees, the oversight of marketing and advertising, and the management of one's own time.

Success Strategies For Managing A Small Business

Make a plan for your business

A successful business plan will clearly state goals and objectives and briefly describe the company and its offerings. Describe the market you intend to join, your sales and marketing strategies, and financial forecasts. Managers of small businesses would do well to assess their company's progress toward its stated objectives periodically.

Keep Your Business And Private Finances Separate

Since your personal and commercial tax obligations are calculated independently, you should maintain two distinct checking accounts for all business-related activities.

Establish How Much Money Is Needed

A startup's financial plan should focus on securing enough capital to keep the business running. Knowing the ins and outs of the various funding options available is crucial, whether you're considering a personal investment, angel investment, business incubator, bank loan, or government award.

Recruit Competent Individuals

Motivated, high-energy, trainable employees whose primary goal is achievement rather than financial gain are essential to the growth and success of any firm. Flexible work hours, regular happy hours, and fun team-building exercises are some ways small business owners can keep their best staff around.

Educate Yourself and Your Team

It will take time for even the most creative new hires to learn the ropes at your company and figure out how to use their newfound knowledge to achieve your long-term objectives. For this reason, a small business must continue learning and training its team with enough training. Develop a training program to increase your team's confidence and effectiveness.

Don't Lose Track of Your Money

Monitoring the company's cash flow when it's first established is simple. However, when your company expands, this process can become tedious. This is why having an accountant on staff or getting user-friendly accounting software to assist with budgeting and cost control is important.

Spend Money On Advertising

In a marketplace where big brands are always vying for consumers' attention, it can take a lot of work for small businesses to get their products and services noticed. Before settling on a marketing strategy for your small business, it's important to research the many possibilities available.

Develop The Skill Of Assigning Tasks To Others

Small business entrepreneurs must learn to manage their time effectively. Tasks you don't like performing or could be more excellent at should be delegated to the wonderful personnel you've hired and trained if you want to manage your time effectively.

What Duties Does a Manager of a Small Company Have?

In small businesses, the manager role often rests with the business owners or is entrusted to a designated individual. The effective management of a small company hinges on a diverse spectrum of business acumen. Within this purview, managers are responsible for steering the organization toward its financial objectives while overseeing crucial functions such as staff recruitment, training, and evaluation. Several pivotal roles underscore the essence of a small business manager's responsibilities:

1. Recruitment, Training, and Education: The initial responsibility entails discovering, recruiting, and nurturing new employees. The manager must ensure a seamless onboarding process and provide continuous education to facilitate staff growth.

2. Inventory Management and Procurement: The discerning selection of inventory and adept management of stock levels fall within the manager's domain. Strategic purchasing decisions contribute to maintaining a balanced and efficient supply chain.

3. Day-to-day Operations: The operational core of the company is within the manager's purview. Overseeing day-to-day functions with precision ensures smooth functionality, contributing to overall success.

4. Financial Objective Fulfillment: A cornerstone responsibility lies in aligning the company's endeavors with its financial targets. The manager

steers the ship towards these objectives, navigating financial waters with prudence.

5. Operational Efficiency: Maintaining an environment of operational excellence is paramount. The manager establishes protocols and systems that uphold efficiency and consistency in daily operations.

6. Budgeting and Expenditure Management: The creation and meticulous execution of the company's financial plan is key. By judiciously managing expenditures, the manager ensures fiscal stability.

7. Sales Target Setting and Monitoring: Formulating sales goals and monitoring progress towards their achievement are pivotal. A manager's adeptness in this domain can greatly influence the company's success.

8. Production, Sales, and Administrative Oversight: Overarching management of production processes, sales strategies, and administrative functions forms a core aspect. Effective coordination of these facets sustains seamless operations.

To be efficacious in this role, a small business manager must adeptly balance time, foster productive staff relationships, and prudently allocate resources. Indeed, the bedrock of any flourishing establishment, particularly within smaller enterprises, is adept and visionary administration. At some juncture, this fundamental realization underpins every company's journey, regardless of size.

Leveraging Technology for Financial Gain

When people and businesses of all income levels can access banking and other financial services, they must thrive. We say that we have achieved financial inclusion. The destitute and the unemployed have little choice but to participate in what is known as the underground or informal economy.

They save what they can, borrow what they need, and manage their day-to-day costs. However, they must resort to unofficial financial management methods because they need access to conventional services like banks, savings accounts, and insurance. Sometimes, the available options need to be expanded and more dangerous. Organizations must embrace digital technology in finance to simplify everyday monetary transactions and advance financial inclusion initiatives.

Increasing financial inclusion initiatives requires better access to the Internet. Therefore, businesses must fortify variables like regulation and compliance standards interacting with technology. Making digital technologies useful for the underprivileged can benefit from this. Digital projects, when carried out correctly, make available to people of varying financial means a wide range of payment, credit, and insurance options. In addition, these services can be provided at a reasonable price for the client. People with access to digital technologies for financial inclusion can better plan for the future, deal with unexpected changes in their income, maintain a steady cash flow, and use their savings toward improving their education, health, or business. Let's examine the advantages of digital technology in financial inclusion. Customers now have access to financial products and services offered by unconventional financial institutions such as non-banking entities and mobile network operators (MNOs). In addition, they can provide financial institutions with services, including data analytics, payment processing, and credit rating.

The way people assess their financial status is changing dramatically due to technological advancements. In particular, it allows the economically disadvantaged to use technology to improve their life. The most obvious way for the economically disadvantaged to benefit from technology is through work and job hunting. Many companies now post their job openings online rather than in traditional media like newspapers or magazines.

Websites like LinkedIn make contacting prospective employers simple for those looking for jobs. Using these channels saves job seekers time and effort while increasing their chances of landing an ideal position. In addition to helping people find employment, the Internet has given rise to online markets where various commodities and services may be bought and sold. Users can open virtual shops on these platforms, exposing their wares to a wider audience. Additionally, they have the option to promote their offerings on social media channels such as Twitter and Facebook. Sellers can leverage these digital marketplaces to reduce rent, utilities, and inventory expenses, all while generating profits.

New business models made possible by technological advancements are lowering the entry barrier for would-be entrepreneurs. Crowdfunding is just one example of a tech-based platform many entrepreneurs use to raise money for their businesses. They can access capital they otherwise would not have had through more conventional means such as bank loans or venture capital. Furthermore, several web-based tools help users set up online shops quickly and efficiently. People can now take advantage of several savings and investment options made possible by technological advancements. Numerous banking apps, for instance, enable people to keep tabs on their finances, plan budgets, and even make stock and other investment purchases. The accounts of many people can be accessed online and safely through the websites or apps of various financial institutions. This paves the way for people to handle their financial matters independently of time and place.

Technological advancements empower the economically disadvantaged by providing them with digital resources for budgeting and planning. These days, it's possible to find an app for just about anything, including budgeting tools like cost tracking, goal setting, and assistance with investing in stocks, bonds, and mutual funds. People can save money by shopping online for the best prices on goods and services using various technological tools. There is no denying that technological advancements have opened up previously unimaginable doorways to economic success for the world's impoverished. These individuals can expand their income streams and improve their financial situations by using online resources such as employment boards, banking apps, and financial planning software. In addition, the availability of digital resources equips people to manage their resources and build a more secure future for themselves and their families. Poor people can improve their economic circumstances with time and effort spent learning to use these resources properly.

Reimagining Education Opportunities

Providing knowledge, skills, and opportunities for individual growth and achievement through education plays a crucial role in shaping people and civilizations. Traditional educational approaches are, however, encountering more and more difficulties in today's society, which is continually expanding. Reimagining educational opportunities is essential to fulfilling the needs of a dynamic and linked global environment. This eBook examines cutting-edge methods and game-changing concepts to empower students and prepare them for the future. Any nation that wishes to overcome poverty and advance must prioritize education. The absence of quality education is devastatingly affecting most African nations. This is true, and it's especially true for the poor and those in need. The government must take several measures to enhance and expand access to education.

A collaborative effort from educators, legislators, parents, and communities is necessary to reimagine educational options. We can unleash learners' full potential and prepare them for future opportunities and challenges by embracing personalized learning, utilizing technology, offering experiential education, emphasizing holistic development, creating flexible learning environments, rethinking assessment methods, empowering educators, and advocating for supportive policies. Together, we can redesign education and create a revolutionary learning ecosystem that encourages creativity, cultivates a passion for lifelong learning, and equips people with the skills they need to succeed in a constantly shifting environment. The opportunities are endless, and education may become more effective.

The Importance of Depoliticizing Education: Fostering Productivity and Growth

Poverty can be eradicated with the help of education. Educated people are more likely to get jobs, make more money, and give back to their communities. Additionally, education can aid people in acquiring critical thinking and problem-solving abilities that will enable them to overcome obstacles and effect change in their communities and lives. Education can also result in better living conditions, better nutrition, and more access to healthcare. Ending the cycle of poverty can be made easier by improving the overall well-being and health of people and communities. It's vital to remember that eliminating poverty might not be possible with just education. Developing young people's minds into well-rounded, critical thinkers capable of advancing their communities is the cornerstone upon which societies create bright futures. However, ideological objectives and polarizing dialogue can eclipse its primary goal when education is politicized. We will analyze the adverse consequences of turning education into a political issue and argue in favor of removing political influences from it. Additionally, we will stress the importance of doing away with politically motivated ideas and making sure that schools do not only serve as indoctrination factories for political ideologies or goals.

The Role Of Education As A Productivity And Growth Catalyst:

Innovation, economic growth, and social advancement are all sped up by education, which acts as a potent growth catalyst for both individual and societal growth. Education enables people to engage productively in the workforce by giving them the knowledge, skills, and critical thinking abilities they need, which boosts production and advances the nation's economy. Depoliticizing education makes it possible to concentrate on giving pupils practical knowledge, stimulating creativity, promoting entrepreneurial thinking, boosting output, and spurring economic growth.

Biased Perspectives Are One Of The Drawbacks Of Politicizing Education.

The danger of offering skewed viewpoints and biased facts increases when education is politicized. The objectivity and legitimacy of the educational system are compromised when some ideas or theories are included or excluded depending on political considerations. This skewed method restricts pupils' capacity for independent information evaluation and critical thought, impeding their overall growth. The politicization of education frequently results in the erosion of academic freedom because educators may feel pressured to follow a specific political narrative or avoid bringing up certain subjects. Diverse viewpoints are suppressed, which stifles intellectual curiosity, prevents open discussion, and prevents the quest for information, all of which are essential for a successful educational environment.

Eliminating Politically Motivated Theories

Objective information Pursuit:

Education should be based on objective inquiry and the pursuit of information, not political objectives. Politically motivated theories compromise the integrity of education by elevating ideology over fact-based study and critical examination. We can ensure that students receive an education founded on facts, evidence, and careful analysis by eliminating such theories, which will encourage them to think critically and make wise judgments. Depoliticizing education allows for the cultivation of intellectual pluralism, which promotes the examination of other points of view and ideas. Students gain empathy, critical thinking abilities, and the capacity to participate in productive debates through exposure to many points of view. This diverse approach allows students to develop well-rounded viewpoints, question presumptions, and better grasp complicated subjects.

Schools should be focused on delivering a balanced curriculum covering various subjects, including history, literature, science, mathematics, and the arts. Schools should be centers of learning, not indoctrination. Instead of indoctrinating kids with a certain political ideology, presenting diverse viewpoints and challenging them to think critically is crucial. Students can establish their own opinions based on a thorough study of various subjects by keeping schools as impartial places. Fostering Active Citizenship: Rather than indoctrination, schools should emphasize encouraging active citizenship by giving students the knowledge and abilities they need to participate properly in democracies. This includes fostering a grasp of democratic procedures, encouraging respectful discussion, and promoting civic values. Students who are given the tools to think critically and independently about political problems are better prepared to participate in society as knowledgeable individuals who can make well-informed decisions.

Funding Augmentation:

The education systems of most developed nations receive substantial government financing. They recognize the importance of a solid education to their personal growth and professional success. Free public education is offered to all citizens in countries like the United States. Most of Africa needs this kind of infrastructure. These nations have never progressed because of inadequate investment. While the United States and other developed countries have several schools providing free tuition to low-income students, developing countries have far fewer options. Therefore, more impoverished young people should have access to school by increasing government financing for education. As a result, Africa will have a brighter future with more opportunities for people with advanced degrees.

Enhancing Existing Facilities:

In developing regions, such as Africa, many poor and underprivileged are concentrated in rural areas with inadequate access to education. The African countries hit by the Boko Haram insurgency can attest to this. These kids often need more than a safe place to study and books and supplies. Because of this, the government should provide resources to construct more educational facilities. As a result, these kids can go to school, and their communities will flourish.

Cleaning Up The System:

Since corruption permeates many African administrations, many African countries' sectors need to be better administered. This corruption, especially pervasive in African countries, can also be seen in education. Several reports of incidents involving special test centers, extortion, and leaked examinations have negatively affected the country's education system. This is because those in authority in these fields seek only to advance their interests. The outcome is dishonest dealings that lower standards in the classroom. Because those from economically disadvantaged families cannot pay for these credentials, they are often overlooked and denied access to school opportunities.

Facilitating Opportunity Sharing:

The vast majority of African countries are categorized as "third world," which denotes a significant wealth disparity between the richest citizens and the rest of the populace. The wealthy get priority regarding schooling options, while the less fortunate are sometimes overlooked. This holds even if more talented young people are drawn to help those in greater need. It is especially evident when students from lower socio-economic backgrounds apply for jobs and are subsequently rejected. This makes it more difficult for low-income families to provide for their children's education. Therefore, it is crucial to work toward greater educational parity.

Organizing Academic Gatherings:

Conferences involving all relevant educational authorities and stakeholders should be held in every country. This will allow them to collaborate on finding long-term answers to urgent issues. Such changes can enhance education and make it possible for more disadvantaged kids to go to school. They can also use this opportunity to introduce new approaches to learning and refresh course materials. For instance, because it was written in 1981, Nigeria's curriculum needs to be updated. The world has changed dramatically since then, and it's a waste for public school children to be taught about obsolete material. Therefore, educational conferences are a viable long-term option for addressing these issues.

How Does College Impact Low-Income?

Many people believe that education is the key to surviving in today's world and thriving in it. Because of this, getting a good education is widely seen as the best way out of poverty. Getting an education can break the cycle of poverty that affects individuals, families, and entire communities. A good education helps kids grow up with better social, emotional, mental, and linguistic abilities. People who go to school learn a lot of useful information and typically learn more advanced skills than those who don't. They can put their newfound knowledge to work by getting better-paying jobs and generally bettering their life. Approximately 171 million people might be lifted out of extreme poverty if all pupils in low-income nations possessed basic reading abilities (but no other skills). The world's poverty rate might be reduced by more than half if all adults had completed secondary school. Because of this, ensuring access to high-quality education is one of the United Nations' Sustainable Development Goals.

The Link Between Education And Economic Development

The value added by expanding one's horizons of understanding is one way in which education contributes to economic growth. Education is the process of imparting knowledge and skills to students in either a classroom setting or one-on-one. For instance, if you want to become an engineer, you'll have to go to school and undergo training, tests, and other practical and theoretical lessons designed to increase your knowledge. After completing this formal education, the graduate will contribute to economic growth by applying what they've learned to a variety of projects that will provide dividends for the economy.

A strong connection exists between a well-educated populace and the discovery of new avenues for income development. For instance, a significantly lower ratio of educated individuals in third-world nations compared to the percentage of educated people in rich countries may prevent most people from developing models that will help them successfully productively utilize their resources. Constant power outages and a lack of power in specific parts of the community are the results of a lack of sufficient infrastructure to support the efficient distribution of energy. Low Gross Domestic Product (GDP) is a common outcome in areas where this is the case because of the negative impact on a country's ability to generate.

Because it correlates with a flourishing economy, education is the most effective means of escaping poverty. Seventy-five percent of the worldwide GDP growth between 1960 and 2000 was related to better math and science skills, according to research published in 2021 by Stanford University and Munich's Ludwig Maximilian University. Knowledge capital, or a country's total stock of brainpower, has been linked to higher economic growth over the long term. Since 1990, many other studies have been released that draw similar conclusions on the correlation between education and economic development.

Equal Access To A High-Quality Education Can Help Eliminate Inequalities

Good education "may be liberating for individuals and can function as a leveler and equalizer throughout society," according to an Oxfam report published in 2019. Inequality contributes significantly to the prevalence of poverty. Extremely poor people are disproportionately affected by marginalization due to systemic restrictions (such as physical ability, religion, race, and caste). Quality education is a fundamental human right, and it may be a powerful tool in the fight against the structural inequalities that put some groups of people at the bottom of the socio-economic ladder. Gender inequality, for instance, is a major factor contributing to the vicious cycle of poverty. Improving the status of women in the classroom has a trickle-down effect on society at large. Concern implemented a version of this, called Community-Based Education, in Afghanistan, and it was a huge success. This is especially important for females because it allows them to attend school in their local communities if they live in rural locations.

Having More Education Is Associated With Lower Rates Of Maternal And Infant Mortality

Regarding women, higher education levels correlate to better maternal and infant health. World Bank and International Center for Research on Women researchers looked at 15 nations in sub-Saharan Africa. They found that educated women had fewer children and had them later in life. In most cases, this results in a more positive outcome for the woman and her children, including safer pregnancies and healthier infants. This link has been empirically verified in Peru. The maternal death rate has decreased by more than 70 percent since 1993, when an adjustment to obligatory schooling rules was enacted, according to research published in 2017. Increasing educational opportunities for girls has been shown to lessen the risk of problems during pregnancy by as much as 29 percent.

Stunting Rates Are Evenly Reduced By Education

Several studies have revealed a correlation between maternal education and reduced incidence of stunting in their children. Children whose growth is stunted because of a lack of nutrients in their initial years of life are more likely to experience various developmental problems later in life. One study found that stunting was prevalent among children in Bangladesh at a rate of 50.7%. However, lower stunting rates were found in populations where both mothers and fathers had high levels of schooling. This correlation was also shown in research conducted in Nairobi, Kenya, showing that children whose mothers had completed some secondary education were 29% less likely to be stunted. Children not stunted in childhood have a 22% higher lifetime earnings potential than their peers. They also tend to produce healthier offspring.

Weakness To Climate Change And Natural Cataclysm

Education is essential in minimizing vulnerability and risk when extreme weather occurrences rise due to climate change. "It is discovered that more educated persons are better aware of the earthquake danger... and are more likely to undertake disaster preparations," Ecology and Society reported in its 2014 issue. There may be a link between education and risk-awareness practices that help people become less vulnerable. The article's authors elaborate by saying that those with higher levels of education are more likely to have a financial safety net to compensate for disaster-related losses, greater access to information about how to prepare for disasters, and a larger social network to lean on during difficult times.

Education Lessens Domestic And Community Violence.

World Bank and ICRW report that demonstrated the link between education and maternal health also demonstrated that the likelihood of child marriage decreased with each additional year of secondary school. Women with higher levels of education have a lower risk of experiencing gender-based violence, particularly from a spouse, because they marry and have children later in life. Girls educated to their full potential are less likely to be subjected to harmful cultural practices like female genital mutilation (FGM). They can better advocate for themselves at home and in the community.

CHAPTER FOUR

INNOVATIVE STRATEGIES FOR NATIONS TO FOSTER WEALTH CREATION

The pressing issue of dire poverty commands immediate attention, casting its harrowing shadows over the lives of countless individuals in developing nations. This multifaceted concern manifests through a spectrum of adversities: insufficient sustenance, substandard shelter, water scarcity, limited literacy, alarming rates of newborn and maternal mortality, burgeoning unemployment, and an overwhelming sense of powerlessness. These are the evident outcomes of a condition that urgently necessitates rectification.

The quest for meaningful change extends through a tapestry of solutions that share a common thread: the empowerment of individuals and communities. A transformative route lies in the promotion of entrepreneurship and microfinance initiatives designed to dismantle the barriers obstructing innovation and the growth of small-scale enterprises. These endeavors infuse hope and capital, driving economic dynamism at the grassroots level.

Furthermore, the cultivation and enhancement of marketing systems form pivotal constituents of the strategy for positive change. By facilitating market access, these systems catalyze economic participation, amplify trade avenues, and augment the visibility of products forged by those at the heart of economic resurgence.

Amidst these endeavors, a cornerstone principle remains unwavering: prioritizing the fundamental needs of the underprivileged within national development policies. This commitment acknowledges the symbiotic relationship between social equity and sustainable progress, propelling inclusive growth.

In tandem with these measures, invigorating the economy emerges as a cornerstone to uplift poverty-ridden communities. Heightened economic activity fuels income growth, thus broadening the spectrum of employment prospects accessible to the marginalized segments of society.

To synthesize, the blueprint for alleviating poverty is forged from multifarious efforts orchestrated in harmony. By championing entrepreneurship, invigorating microfinance, enhancing market accessibility, embedding equity in development policies, and catalyzing economic growth, we sow the seeds of change. As these strategies intertwine and flourish, the trajectory of poverty undergoes a radical shift, and the marginalized find themselves journeying toward empowerment, resilience, and hope.

Establishing an Enabling Atmosphere for Investment and Expansion of Businesses

Sustainable development is the practice of ensuring that current and future generations both have enough resources to live comfortably. It's founded on the belief that sustainable development requires balancing economic expansion, social progress, and environmental safeguards. To ensure that the Earth and its resources will be accessible to future generations, sustainable development is crucial. It fosters more equal communities by lowering poverty and raising living standards.

In addition to fostering innovation and efficiency and generating new avenues for business, sustainable development can boost GDP growth. Climate change, biodiversity decline, pollution, and resource exhaustion are just a handful of the challenges to sustainable development. Overcoming these challenges requires collaborative efforts from governments, businesses, civil society, and individuals and implementing enduring sustainable policies and practices.

Among the Sustainable Development Goals (SDGs) embraced by the United Nations within the 2030 Agenda for Sustainable Development framework, one is dedicated to guaranteeing universal access to quality employment and fostering economic growth for all individuals. The mission is to advance economic growth that benefits all full and productive employment and good work for all. This entails expanding access to higher-quality employment opportunities, enhancing existing ones, and bolstering universal social safety nets. The target also includes helping local firms and entrepreneurs succeed while decreasing poverty and income disparity.

Policies focusing on development aim to foster long-term, broad-based economic expansion. These measures can potentially improve global resource efficiency and offer decent employment opportunities. Governments, businesses, and other organizations may all do their part to eliminate unemployment and boost economic growth by enacting development-oriented policies. The Sustainable Development Goals (SDGs) encompass a collection of worldwide targets that can be promoted by reducing poverty and inequality while enhancing prosperity for all individuals, regardless of location.

A government that has Equal compensation for equal effort, full and productive employment opportunities for all men and women Equal compensation for equal effort, full and productive employment opportunities for all genders, including youth and those with impairments. The government needs to significantly lower the number of young people who are neither working nor in school or training. There is a need to establish regulations to expand micro, small, and medium-sized businesses by expanding their access to capital.

To better assist developing nations in increasing their capacities, especially the least developed nations and tiny island developing states, it is important to abolish all types of child labor, including recruiting and employing child soldiers. Urgent and efficient measures need to be implemented to eliminate forced labor, put an end to contemporary slavery and human trafficking, and ensure the eradication of the most severe instances of child labor. This is done to safeguard the rights of all employees, particularly those in temporary or unstable employment, migrants, and especially female migrants while promoting safe and secure working conditions for everyone.

The goal is to make it easier for domestic financial institutions to provide the general public with banking, insurance, and other financial services. Eliminating poverty and promoting economic growth in nations requires an atmosphere conducive to investment and corporate expansion. When countries develop suitable circumstances for investment, they attract money, boost entrepreneurship, generate employment opportunities, and stimulate economic growth.

In this response, I will discuss some of the most effective policies and programs countries may use to foster this atmosphere. Investing is much easier if the government is trustworthy and things run smoothly. Countries must create open and accountable institutions, uphold the rule of law, and fight corruption. A secure political climate instills trust among investors and safeguards private property. Investment-friendly laws and regulations that streamline administrative processes are something all countries should implement. Both domestic and international investors might be enticed by cutting red tape and improving administrative efficiency.

In addition, establishing a policy framework that is stable and predictable encourages long-term investment. Businesses can only thrive with sufficient utilities, roads, communications, and storage facilities. Governments should invest in infrastructure projects to increase trade, lower transportation costs, and open new markets. This improves the country's appeal as an investment destination by facilitating the smooth flow of commodities and lowering production costs.

In order to promote corporate expansion, it is essential to set up a solid financial structure. Governments should ease the process of obtaining funding for businesses, especially those classified as "small" and "medium" (SMEs). This can be accomplished through expanding financial services, including banking, and creating credit guarantee programs. Businesses can grow, innovate, and create new jobs with easier financing access. A well-educated and talented labor force is essential to encourage investment and expand existing businesses. Countries should put more money into education and vocational training to produce skilled workers. The availability of qualified people can be increased by encouraging education in STEM fields, which can encourage innovation and entrepreneurship.

Inspiring creative problem-solving and entrepreneurial spirit can boost the economy and create new jobs. Governments can encourage innovation by funding R&D, granting tax breaks to businesses that rely on new ideas, and encouraging partnerships between universities and private companies. Business accelerators, incubators, and technology parks can all help new companies get off the ground. Liberalizing trade and lowering trade barriers can entice investors and stimulate the economy. All nations should actively pursue free trade policies, lower trade barriers, and streamline customs procedures. Two benefits of joining regional trade agreements and global value chains are increased market access and competitiveness.

For poverty reduction and broad economic growth, it is essential to fund social infrastructure like healthcare, schools, and safety nets. The social stability of a society and its attractiveness to investors can be improved by addressing fundamental human needs and narrowing wealth gaps. The advantages of economic progress should be evenly distributed, and social safety nets can help do just that. Infrastructure development and economic progress can be propelled by public-private partnerships thanks to the pooling of resources and knowledge. Governments may ease the way for PPPs by establishing a friendly legal environment, guaranteeing equitable risk-sharing procedures, and encouraging sustainability. Public-private partnerships (PPPs) help nations attract private investment while delivering core public services effectively.

Keeping the economy stable is essential to encourage investment and expansion. Inflation and financial instability can be avoided if nations implement sensible fiscal and monetary policies. It is easier for firms to plan and invest in projects with a long time horizon when the local currency is stable, and financing rates are competitive. Political stability, supportive policies, infrastructure development, access to finance, human capital development, innovation, market liberalization, social infrastructure investment, and macroeconomic stability are all necessary components of an environment conducive to investment and business growth. Countries can combat poverty, boost economic growth, and enhance the living conditions of their population by adopting these policies.

Why Nations Should Consider Glocalization

Globalization refers to a good or service designed for a worldwide audience but tailored to meet buyers' needs in certain regions. Automobiles are a common example of a product sold on a global scale but modified to satisfy local conditions, such as emissions standards or where the driver's seat is positioned. A global fast-food business, for example, can provide regionally or linguistically distinct menu items in different regions to appeal to local palates. Media and advertising initiatives sensitive to local customs are a common part of glocalization efforts, which aim to increase the popularity of imported goods.

While glocalization can assist international businesses in tailoring their offerings to local markets, it also comes with the risk of cultural appropriation. Companies with a decentralized authority structure operating in and competing across numerous cultural contexts benefit the most from glocalization. Although costly and time-consuming, businesses that invest in this strategy typically reap the benefits of reaching customers in a wider range of cultural contexts. It also strengthens the competitiveness of those businesses in certain sectors. Some have argued that glocalization is a response to the criticism that globalization leads to cultural uniformity. One way to look at glocalization is as the antithesis of Americanization, or the process by which another country's culture is influenced by American culture and business (also known as "McDonaldization").

What Does it Mean to Globalize?

The term 'glocalization' refers to the process by which a multinational organization alters some of its services or products to suit better the needs and preferences of a specific local market—a combination of the terms 'global' and 'local.' There are numerous types of glocalization. For instance, in the United Kingdom, manufacturers must install steering wheels on the right side of automobiles. Similarly, foods are adapted in many nations to suit regional palates better. Alongside the standard fare of hamburgers and chicken items, fast-food restaurants like McDonald's Corporation (MCD) and others will often offer regional specialties.

Campaigns to improve the public's perception of a company are also conducted in local languages and take into account cultural norms and practices. Corporations have been driving the process of globalization, which involves the movement of goods, ideas, and money across national boundaries. Globalization has been criticized because it can potentially reduce cultural diversity and make customers more alike. Glocalization considers regional norms and values to tailor goods and services to specific markets.

The overall economic effects of glocalization attempts have varied. Glocalization, which helps multinational corporations compete more effectively with domestic firms, should boost competition and decrease prices, making goods more widely available. Smaller local firms might be negatively impacted by glocalization due to the low manufacturing costs of larger corporations. This is because huge multinational corporations are typically the ones engaging in glocalization. Because of this, there may be less competition, leading to higher pricing.

Deceptions about Globalization

Some opponents of globalization argue that multinational firms' ability to operate freely across national boundaries is inherently corrupt. In their eyes, multinational firms only care about evading taxes and paying exploitation wages. However, the data contradicts these broad statements, showing that countries that are successful at attracting FDI have higher real salaries and higher corporate tax collections. Additionally, the presence of internationally active corporations produces tremendous incentives to swiftly enhance local standards in management, technology, and environmental quality, thereby allowing the host country to participate more effectively in globalization. In my opinion, most multinational corporations act ethically. There are, of course, exceptions, but they should be treated as such. Even while its staunchest opponents cling to illusions about globalization, the richest countries are responsible for most of the growth in international investment and commerce.

Just over 20% of overall FDI was invested in developing nations in 2017, whereas developing countries only accounted for 27% of global exports of manufactured goods. This includes the six major Southeast Asian exporters. The longer developing countries need to catch up, the more difficult it is for their businesses to compete globally because of global supply networks' increasing sophistication and complexity. There is a widespread understanding among governments, business elites, and average residents in emerging nations that they must fully embrace globalization. According to a recent poll by the World Economic Forum, globalization has the support of the people of nations like China and India. They understand that increased transparency and access to additional opportunities are essential to improving people's quality of life.

There has never been a better opportunity to take advantage of comparative advantage than in today's era of freer commerce. Moreover, trade is a means of importing good policies, as it weakens ineffective and corrupt practices and fosters a more favorable setting for doing business in the countries that participate in it. According to John Stuart Mill's Principles of Political Economy, commerce's intellectual and moral benefits far outweigh the monetary ones.

Benefits of Glocalization

Glocalization, a dynamic approach that seamlessly combines regional customization with global opportunities, brings forth a multitude of advantages for national development. By aligning their operations to local conditions while tapping into the worldwide network of enterprises and services, businesses and organizations can harness a range of benefits:

1. **Regional Adaptation, Global Reach:** Glocalization empowers entities to adapt their strategies to regional nuances, enabling them to navigate specific local dynamics efficiently. Simultaneously, it provides a gateway to leverage global prospects, striking a harmonious balance between local relevance and international scope.

2. **Economic Boost through Foreign Investment**: Embracing glocalization attracts foreign investment, bolstering a nation's economic ecosystem. The tailored approach entices investors with the promise of strategies aligned with local needs, paving the way for economic growth and expansion.

3. **Access to Emerging Markets:** Glocalization unlocks new markets, creating avenues for national businesses to broaden their horizons. The tailored approach resonates with diverse demographics, enabling market penetration and fostering economic diversification.

4. **Enhanced International Competitiveness:** The glocalization paradigm equips local entities to compete globally. Businesses can enhance their competitive edge by tailoring products and services to local preferences while integrating with international trends.

5. **Technological Advancement:** Integrating glocalization enables access to cutting-edge technology from across the globe. This infusion of innovation enriches local industries, propelling national development on technological fronts.

6. **Cultural Enrichment and Cross-Cultural Understanding**: Glocalization nurtures cross-cultural understanding and respect. Bridging cultural divides and fostering interactions between diverse communities contribute to a harmonious society while driving economic progress.

7. International Harmony: Glocalization serves as a conduit for international dialogue and cultural exchange. Through shared experiences and insights, it has the potential to reduce prejudices and promote global harmony.

8. Environmental Sustainability: Glocalization extends its impact on environmental conservation. Encouraging environmentally conscious practices, such as energy-efficient measures and sustainable sourcing, promotes responsible business conduct and contributes to a greener future.

Glocalization is not just a strategy but a powerful instrument that propels national development by capitalizing on local strengths and global opportunities. This harmonious blend enhances economic prosperity, cultural understanding, international harmony, and environmental sustainability, steering nations toward a brighter future.

Methods for Fostering Economic Prosperity

Several methods can be used to advance decent employment and economic expansion. We can build more equitable and prosperous communities by adopting these practices.

There needs to be more jobs, and income inequality is increasing. Allocating resources towards education and training has the potential to result in a more skilled and proficient workforce, an increase in employment opportunities, and elevated living standards. These factors are essential for fostering quality employment and facilitating economic growth. It's a long-term bet because it equips the next generation with the tools they'll need to succeed in the workforce. Investing in education and training can promote decent work and economic growth. This approach has many advantages, including People can see better their employment prospects by investing in their education and training. This is especially helpful for the unemployed, who can boost their employability and job prospects through education and training.

By 2030, 8.9 million more people should be actively looking for work. Investments in education and training will be essential to meeting the requirements of the expanding labor force and generating new jobs. This is especially crucial in developing nations, where a big influx of young people may enter the labor force but need more suitable employment alternatives.

Employees possessing advanced education and training tend to excel in their positions. The effectiveness and competitive edge of companies and institutions can be enhanced through investments in education and training. Some examples of investments in learning are access to education and training opportunities, such as financial support for K-12, higher education, and occupational certification and training. Helping students afford their education and training options is another kind of this. Here are ten steps you can take to improve schooling around the globe.

The quality of education and training can be increased, and teachers can be given the tools they need to teach effectively if countries invest in their professional growth and training.

Depoliticization of Economy

There are many ways in which the government, corporations, and people as a whole could gain from removing politics from economic matters. Business owners, entrepreneurs, and individuals can make decisions unconstrained by short-term policy or personal interests when politics is removed from decision-making. Because of this, they can put their attention where it will do the most good for their companies and the country. When problems are removed from the political sphere, firms are free to make investments without fear of retaliation from elected officials, which can boost the economy. This additional funding can be put toward research and development, worker training, and other programs that promote national output. Businesses will be encouraged to expand and generate new employment due to cheaper taxes and less bureaucracy, which will, in turn, boost the economy.

Small and medium-sized businesses (SMEs) can benefit from depoliticizing economic concerns since they will have easier access to financing, allowing them to grow without fear of political interference. When business owners have easier access to capital, they are better able to study the industry and come up with creative solutions to challenges. Small businesses may benefit from more competition, resulting in cheaper consumer costs.

Overall, depoliticizing economic matters can boost a country's economy in the short and long term by encouraging more investment, job creation, and increased national wealth. Companies of all sizes can get an advantage in the market by using this method to gain access to financing. The country and its people as a whole might benefit from this. Therefore, it is evident that removing politics from economic matters can help the country prosper. Making decisions with the nation's long-term financial health in mind will help firms prioritize their interests, boosting economic growth. All members of society may benefit from this in the long run.

The Pros of Depoliticization of the Economy

The state of Maine's economy must be depoliticized. Our economy is struggling due to many factors, such as a lack of competitiveness with other states, a declining workforce, and high costs for businesses that impede job growth and raise family living expenses. There should be no political or ideological motivations in finding answers to these problems. They must be founded on thorough investigation and accurate data. We may all agree that a robust economy, flourishing communities, and prosperous families in Maine can be attained. Still, to get there, we need solutions from both sides of the aisle that constitute a long-term, comprehensive plan to develop the economy through foundational jobs. Taking politics out of the economy is the best way to remember that we're all in this together. Putting all our faith in one camp and criticizing the other will only fix Maine's economy a little. The Alliance for Maine publishes a newsletter that might help you learn more and keep up with the topics.

Government Should Consider Responsible Deregulation

Deregulation, in which the government's role in an industry is diminished or eliminated, is typically implemented to boost competition. The ongoing debate between those who favor stricter government oversight and those who prefer less interference has changed the market landscape. The finance industry has a long tradition of being one of the most closely examined in the United States. Proponents of deregulation claim that burdensome laws do more harm than good by restricting investment opportunities and slowing economic progress.

Indeed, the stock market crash of 1929 and the subsequent Great Depression led to increased oversight of the financial sector in the United States. In reaction to the most profound financial crisis in the history of the United States, the Roosevelt administration introduced a series of financial regulations. This encompassed significant legislative measures such as the Securities Exchange Acts of 1933 and 1934, alongside the U.S. Banking Act of 1933, often known as the Glass-Steagall Act.

The initiation of the Securities and Exchange Acts was the driving force behind the establishment of the Securities and Exchange Commission (SEC).

The purpose of this regulatory body is to oversee the securities markets and mandate that publicly traded companies disclose crucial financial information. According to the Glass-Steagall Act, a bank couldn't do commercial and investment banking. In order to prevent significant national banks from participating in irresponsible and deceptive activities that could result in unintended consequences for the financial markets, this reform law was established with the belief that these banks need regulations to pursue profits.

For a long time, deregulation advocates have said burdensome laws are counterproductive because they discourage investment and slow economic progress.

Background on Deregulatory Movements

Responsible deregulation is a program in which the government loosens its grip on businesses by lowering existing rules. It's predicated on easing business activity restrictions without compromising consumer protections and the general populace. Increased competition, new employment opportunities, increased innovation, and a quicker economic recovery are all possible outcomes of sensible deregulation.

Increased economic growth in the form of greater earnings, lower pricing for goods and services, fewer taxes, better infrastructure, and more job opportunities is the fundamental advantage of appropriate deregulation. By reducing the number of rules and regulations affecting how businesses operate, we can make the market more competitive, saving money that can be put into growth-oriented activities. Consumption more on company growth and innovation can potentially improve employment and consumer spending.

Responsible deregulation also benefits the environment by motivating firms to act sustainably. When businesses are in competition with one another, they are less likely to waste resources and increase their efficiency and environmental friendliness. In addition, businesses are better able to invest in developing renewable energy sources to replace conventional fossil fuels because of the lighter regulatory load. Overall, appropriate deregulation can preserve public safety and provide a better environment for individuals while helping to increase the economy. Government officials should thoroughly vet any proposed deregulatory initiatives before being put into action. When carried out correctly, deregulation can give an economy growing slowly and high unemployment a much-needed boost.

The Federal Reserve (Fed) revised its interpretation of the Glass-Steagall Act in 1986 to allow commercial banks to earn up to 5% of their total revenue from investment banking. That percentage was raised to 25% in 1996. The Federal Reserve Board legalized underwriting by commercial banks the next year, allowing businesses and governments to access the debt and equity markets.

The implementation of the Riegle-Neal Interstate Banking and Branching Efficiency Act in 1994 triggered modifications to both the Federal Deposit Insurance Act and the Bank Holding Company Act of 1956. Subsequently, in 1999, the Glass-Steagall Act was revoked as a consequence of the Financial Services Modernization Act signed during the Clinton administration.

Furthermore, as a result of the Commodity Futures Modernization Act of 2000, credit default swaps and other OTC derivatives were removed from the regulatory oversight of the Commodity Futures Trading Commission. Additionally, in 2004, the Securities and Exchange Commission (SEC) implemented changes that reduced the compulsory reserve ratio applicable to investment banks.

However, deregulation efforts stopped after the subprime mortgage crisis of 2007 and the subsequent financial catastrophe of 2007-2008, most notably with the passing of the Dodd-Frank Act in 2010, which limited subprime mortgage lending and derivatives trading. However, following the 2016 U.S.

presidential and congressional elections, which saw a Republican majority, then-President Donald Trump and his party directed their efforts toward the repeal of Dodd-Frank.

Dodd-Frank was established to avoid the unexpected collapse of large financial institutions, but in May 2018, Trump signed a law that exempted small and regional banks from its strictest standards. Following extensive deliberations with Democrats, the bill received significant support and was passed with a considerable majority in both chambers of Congress. Before this, President Trump had expressed his intention to alter Dodd-Frank and possibly eliminate it significantly. But former Massachusetts Democrat and bill cosponsor Barney Frank noted, "This is not a significant number on the bill. It's not even a big figure. Major provisions of Dodd-regulations Frank's were not repealed.

How Does Deregulation Affect Things?

The elimination of barriers to entry for new enterprises is one of deregulation's desired outcomes, as is an increase in investment opportunities. As more businesses enter markets and compete with one another, costs for customers tend to decrease. Businesses are better able to invest in R&D when they spend less time and money on regulatory compliance.

If rules don't constrain businesses, they may focus on innovating new products, pricing those items competitively, hiring more people, expanding into new markets, investing in additional assets, and interacting with customers. Which sectors in the United States are the most heavily governed?

The most heavily governed sectors in the USA

In the United States, certain sectors face extensive governance to ensure compliance and operational integrity. The following list outlines the sectors that experience the highest levels of regulation:

1. Electrical Power: The production, transmission, and distribution of electrical power are tightly regulated to guarantee safety, reliability, and accessibility.

2. Vehicle Manufacturing: Vehicle assembly plants adhere to stringent regulations to ensure the quality, safety, and environmental responsibility of the automobiles they produce.

3. Petroleum and Coal Products: Regulations in the production of goods derived from petroleum and coal encompass safety measures, environmental preservation, and quality control.

4. Scheduled Air Travel: The aviation industry, specifically scheduled air travel, is subject to rigorous oversight to safeguard passenger safety and maintain operational excellence.

5. Fishing: Regulatory measures in the fishing industry are designed to maintain sustainable practices, prevent overfishing, and protect aquatic ecosystems.

6. Non-Bank Credit Intermediation: Entities engaged in credit intermediation outside of traditional banks operate within a regulated framework to ensure fair practices and financial stability.

7. Banking Credit Mediation: Banks providing credit mediation services are subject to regulations that foster sound financial operations, consumer protection, and economic stability.

8. Oil and Gas Extraction: The extraction of oil and gas is governed by regulations focused on safety, environmental preservation, and responsible resource utilization.

9. **Navigation in Maritime and Great Lakes:** The maritime sector, including navigation on the open sea, shores, and the Great Lakes, operates within strict guidelines to ensure navigational safety and prevent environmental harm.

10. **Pharmaceutical Processing:** The processing of drugs and pharmaceuticals is closely regulated to ensure product efficacy, patient safety, and adherence to quality standards.

In these sectors, regulations play a crucial role in maintaining safety, promoting responsible practices, and safeguarding stakeholders' interests. These regulations collectively contribute to the well-being of both industries and the broader society.

Can you imagine a world without federal rules in the United States?

Without government oversight, the risks associated with utilizing common products like medication, automobiles, food, and beverages would increase. There would be no guarantee of a risk-free workplace. Employees may be required to work long hours, including weekends and overtime, or risk losing their jobs. For instance, before the Clean Water and Environmental Protection Acts were enacted in 1970, rivers and other bodies of water often became so dirty that they caught fire.

Benefits of Deregulation

Economic expansion is boosted by deregulation. It is believed that productivity will increase by giving businesses more leeway in how they are conducted. No regulations limit the number of hours a day that manufacturers can operate or the materials used in production.

Evading legal expenses allows companies to allocate funds toward hiring more personnel or acquiring advanced machinery. Revenue can be boosted by reducing prices. The process of deregulation has resulted in heightened competition and decreased pricing within sectors like transportation and communications. Additionally, deregulation diminishes obstacles to market entry, which is advantageous for startups by minimizing their operational expenses. Operating expenses decrease, enabling new businesses to enter the market and lowering prices for consumers. These factors can enhance productivity and drive economic expansion.

Helping Out Small Business Owners

Facilitating the success of small businesses holds significant importance for the overall economy, fostering job creation and yielding advantages for all. Nonetheless, small enterprises often need help accessing resources such as capital and markets. One of the main causes of a company's collapse is a shortage of capital. This can exacerbate the problem of poor employment prospects, which is especially acute in developing nations. These obstacles can be addressed, and small-scale manufacturing and economic activity can be encouraged if governments, firms, and other organizations adequately assist the sector.

Among the many approaches to helping local enterprises thrive are Microloans and other forms of funding made available through traditional banking channels, which can aid small firms in overcoming this obstacle and allowing them to expand. Businesses can help small businesses by incorporating them into their supply chains and buying goods and services. This can aid in expanding small firms' reach, allowing them to take advantage of increased economic output. Training and assistance programs can help small firms enhance their operations, boost their competitiveness, and adjust to shifts in the labor market.

Improve Working Conditions And Salaries

Promoting economic growth through increased productivity, decreased turnover, fair compensation, and safe and decent working conditions is essential. One way to preserve workers' rights and advance social justice is to guarantee they are compensated fairly and provided with safe and acceptable working conditions. Fair wages and working conditions can be encouraged through various means, such as Setting minimum wage levels and ensuring that workers are adequately compensated for their talents and experience. These are two ways to achieve this goal.

Promoting equitable wages and conditions is especially crucial in labor-intensive industries, where salaries and working conditions impact economic growth. The Economic Policy Institute reports that the likelihood of poverty for domestic employees is three times that of other workers. This is especially crucial in developing nations, where more respectable employment prospects are needed for economic growth.

Workplaces should be safe and without risks, and employees should have access to appropriate safety gear and other resources. Defending employees' freedom to form and join unions and other forms of worker organization is one way to safeguard their rights and interests.

Promote Entrepreneurial Activity

Introducing novel goods, services, and technologies into the market is one way entrepreneurship promotes innovation and economic growth. In numerous developing countries, a substantial portion of the population depends on the informal economy as their means of sustenance. Enhancing the transition of informal economy workers into the formal sector can be achieved by providing educational and training avenues and fostering entrepreneurial endeavors. Among these methods for fostering an entrepreneurial spirit are: The capacity to establish and expand enterprises is hindered when entrepreneurs cannot secure financing. Financing opportunities can help business owners overcome this obstacle and expand their operations.

Support aspiring and established business owners to back initiatives that foster business growth. Business-friendly environments can be fostered when governments and other organizations streamline the company registration process, lighten the regulatory load, and offer other forms of support. Economic growth can be fueled by fostering an environment that encourages the development of novel products, services, and technologies by entrepreneurs. This may include funding experimental endeavors or encouraging the introduction of innovative tools.

Encourage Gender Parity

Women have a higher poverty rate than males in several countries. When women have more opportunities to earn a living wage, it helps to alleviate poverty. Reducing the wage gap between men and women in the workforce has boosted productivity and fueled economic expansion. Young women worldwide are more likely to be unemployed and undereducated than their male counterparts. The workforce benefits from diversity and creating more good jobs when women can enter the workforce on equal terms with men.

It also boosts the number of people who can find work. This has the potential to stimulate the international economy and boost long-term growth. If gender gaps in the workforce were eliminated, global GDP growth could increase by 26%. Increasing output is yet another benefit of promoting gender equality in the workplace. Including women in the workforce has improved critical thinking, creativity, and problem-solving and increased diversity.

Facilitate Commerce

Engaging in international trade enables businesses to expand their global presence and uphold their competitive edge. Governments hold a crucial responsibility in encouraging and streamlining these trade activities, which encompass actions like:

1. Negotiating Trade Agreements: Governments can forge bilateral and multilateral agreements to eliminate tariffs and dismantle trade barriers, fostering smoother international trade relations.

2. Streamlining Domestic-International Trade: Efforts can be directed at facilitating seamless trade between domestic and international markets, simplifying logistics and enhancing efficiency.

3. Trade Assistance: Governments extend support to businesses through trade funding initiatives. Credits, guarantees, and insurance mechanisms are instrumental in mitigating export-related risks, bolstering companies' confidence in venturing into global markets.

4. Navigating Regulations: Technical assistance provided by governments aids firms in navigating the intricacies of international trade regulations. This includes aiding businesses with certification, labeling, and other regulatory requisites.

5. Fostering Business Contacts: Governments sponsor trade missions and events that facilitate networking and connections for companies in international markets. These initiatives offer businesses the platform to forge new contacts, expand their clientele, and explore fresh business horizons.

By leveraging these strategic actions, governments contribute significantly to creating an enabling environment for international trade. This, in turn, empowers businesses to expand their horizons, embrace new opportunities, and remain competitive in the ever-evolving global landscape.

Promote Creativity

Productivity, total employment, new market entry, and product and service creation are all boosted by innovative practices. Moreover, encouraging innovation can motivate productive actions, which in turn can boost GDP (GDP). Insufficient investments in research and development might stunt a country's potential to innovate and develop new technologies. Businesses are more likely to invest in innovative products and processes if governments offer financial incentives.

Several metrics can be used to assess how well a country is encouraging innovation. Among these are metrics like new company formation, R&D funding, and patent applications. The most relevant indicators regarding economic development stage, size, and structure may differ. Thus, it's vital to consider these factors in light of a country's unique national conditions.

Put Money Into Infrastructure

Sustaining economic growth in rural and urban regions necessitates substantial investments in infrastructure development. Examples of such infrastructure encompass transportation networks, communication systems, energy generation, distribution, and water and sanitation facilities. Investment in infrastructure can be especially useful in enhancing connectivity and access to markets in rural areas. For instance, investment in roads and bridges can make it easier for companies to ship their wares and enter new markets.

Sometimes, more help from the private sector or governments is needed to promote innovation. Slower growth, for instance, could be attributable to a need for more access to current technologies and breakthroughs in low-income countries. Investment in new technologies and the Internet of Things, such as artificial intelligence and digital infrastructure, can benefit economic expansion as more conventional forms of physical infrastructure. These innovations can be used across industries to boost productivity, cut costs, and encourage new ideas. Furthermore, funding for new technologies can facilitate technical advancement and propel new ideas.

Encourage Long-Term Growth

Protecting the environment and ensuring the benefits of growth are spread evenly are both possible goals of sustainable economic growth. Addressing global issues like poverty, inequality, and environmental degradation by balancing development's social, economic, and environmental effects is central to sustainable development. Long-term, sustainable increases in GDP and improved living standards for all members of society are possible outcomes of efforts to promote sustainable development. Promoting tourism that is kind to the planet and helpful to locals is an important part of this strategy.

Sustainable tourism benefits both the environment and the host community by lowering the rate of environmental degradation and boosting the economy. In other words, we need to get people to change their consumption habits so they don't end up depleting our natural resources. For instance, environmentally friendly product promotion and local agricultural support can slow the economic and environmental decline. The health of a population is intrinsically tied to sustainable development. Achieving sustainable development is only possible by ensuring everyone can access safe drinking water, nutritious food, and other essentials. The advantages of economic progress can be more evenly distributed with the help of robust institutions and policies that promote health and well-being.

Social Security

Individuals and families particularly susceptible to poverty and social exclusion are the primary beneficiaries of government-funded social safety programs. Unemployment insurance, retirement plans, healthcare, and schooling are all examples of such schemes. Social protection measures can lessen the severity of poverty and strengthen the economy by assisting unemployed people. This helps to encourage the creation of good jobs and makes it easier for companies to put money into the economy.

The fruits of economic prosperity should be spread everywhere, and social protection measures can do just that. Social protection programs can minimize income inequality and foster social cohesion by providing low-income individuals and families with a safety net. As a result, there will be less likely social unrest and basic social contract deterioration, which can provide a more stable and sustainable economy. Social protection programs can aid in lowering environmental degradation and increasing sustainable consumption by assisting vulnerable individuals and families. As a result, firms may feel more encouraged to invest and expand, thereby boosting the economy by creating high-quality jobs.

Long-term economic growth and sustainable international leadership are possible if countries prioritize social protection. Therefore, meeting people's basic needs should be at the heart of any international plan to boost the economy. A diversified strategy that considers the requirements of both enterprises and individuals is necessary to promote decent work and economic progress. Countries can achieve long-term, sustainable economic growth by implementing these policies, leading to a rise in the number of good employment available, productivity, and competitiveness. The social, economic, and environmental implications of development must be considered together by governments, enterprises, and other stakeholders if economic growth is to be achieved sustainably. Humanity stands to gain from a more prosperous and equitable global economy, which they can help bring about by working together in this way.

Deconcentration of the Economy

The deconcentration of the economy has recently garnered increasing attention, sparking discussions about reshaping economic activities beyond traditional epicenters and urban hubs. This notion's fundamental premise is to elevate living standards, bolster national wealth, and broaden resource accessibility across the country. This transformative shift might involve relocating manufacturing facilities from suburban areas to city centers, reconfiguring shipping routes around congested transportation nodes, and revitalizing overlooked regions. The profound potential of deconcentration extends far beyond mere economic redistribution; it holds the promise of fostering inclusivity, empowering marginalized segments, and generating a more equitable and dynamic economic landscape.

Promoting Equitable Participation

Deconcentration seeks to diffuse economic activities at its core, ensuring that the benefits are shared irrespective of geographical location. This democratization of economic advantages holds the potential to curtail income disparities, spur job creation, and amplify resource availability on a broader scale. An illustrative example could be the relocation of factories from urban cores to outlying areas, consequently affording rural inhabitants better access to goods and services previously beyond their reach. This approach narrows economic gaps and enhances the quality of life for those who have long been economically marginalized.

Unlocking Global Opportunities

The strategic rerouting of commerce away from congested ports or airports is another facet of deconcentration. This redirection opens new vistas for local manufacturers and product exporters, enabling them to tap into global markets that were hitherto inaccessible due to infrastructure constraints. As economic activities diversify and disperse, businesses gain the latitude to experiment with novel technologies and cost-effective inputs. This experimentation often paves the way for heightened innovation, whereby businesses discover more efficient and lucrative production methods, consequently propelling economic growth.

Empowering Overlooked Economies

Deconcentration also holds transformative potential for neglected local economies, particularly small towns or rural areas. Historically sidelined due to their distance from major cities, these regions can emerge as thriving investment and production hubs if provided the opportunity to attract economic activity away from traditional urban centers. This shift could precipitate an upswing in local earnings and employment prospects, thereby contributing to poverty reduction. By redistributing economic vitality, deconcentration becomes a formidable tool for invigorating economies hampered by geographical or physical limitations, fostering greater resource access, and catalyzing fresh avenues for corporate ingenuity.

Leveling the Economic Playing Field

The impact of deconcentration transcends economic metrics, encompassing socio-economic dimensions such as income distribution and resource availability. The proverbial playing field can be leveled by dispersing economic activity from metropolitan cores, enabling a more balanced distribution of income and resources. This, in turn, elevates the standard of living for a wider cross-section of the populace. As regions beyond urban hubs garner economic momentum, they cease to be relegated to the peripheries, evolving into vibrant centers of enterprise and opportunity.

A Path to Prosperity

In an era marked by dynamic shifts in global economies, deconcentration emerges as a potent strategy for nations aiming to augment their standard of living. By embracing deconcentration, nations can transcend historical limitations and geographical constraints, ushering in a new era of economic inclusivity and dynamism. The transformational potential of deconcentration is far-reaching, offering a promising trajectory toward prosperity, innovation, and equitable economic growth. It's a tangible testament to the fact that economic vitality need not be confined to urban enclaves; rather, it has the power to bloom across diverse landscapes, enriching lives and forging a more balanced and prosperous future for all.

Nurturing Competitive Industries

In economic advancement, a dynamic interaction unfolds between governments and businesses, forging a symbiotic partnership that propels progress, innovation, and vitality. Governments wield a decisive influence over the economic landscape, shaping an environment conducive to small and large businesses' growth and sustenance.

A potent instrument within the government's arsenal is the ability to shape interest rates. The Federal Reserve holds the authority to adjust the Federal Funds Target Rate, directly impacting the prime interest rate. This adjustment triggers a cascade of economic effects, where a lower prime rate fosters a favorable atmosphere for borrowing, catalyzing business expansion and bolstering disposable income for consumers.

Going beyond conventional wisdom, the government's tax toolkit comprises an array of strategic measures that can catalyze the growth of specific industries. Tax breaks tailored to targeted enterprises or consumers within specific sectors are potentially transformative. A vivid example lies in the burgeoning commercial and household solar power sectors. Tailored tax incentives support solar power startups and empower them to embark on innovative trajectories.

International trade stands as a linchpin of economic vitality, with governments acting as architects of a trade-friendly environment. By recalibrating tax structures and dismantling import barriers, governments cultivate an ecosystem conducive to international trade. This has a ripple effect on local businesses, reducing trade obstacles and establishing free-trade zones. The outcome is a landscape that yields advantages ranging from cost savings for local enterprises to expanded operational capacities.

Strategic collaborations between governments and private enterprises wield transformative influence. Such partnerships inject economic vigor into various sectors. Through engagement with external entities, governments optimize resource allocation and streamline operations. For instance, counties can circumvent the creation of new divisions by contracting external companies for tasks like road construction and snow clearance.

By pooling tax revenues, governments wield a powerful instrument to stimulate economic transformation. These pooled resources catalyze entrepreneurship through tailored loan and support programs for aspiring business owners. Organizations like the Small Business Administration exemplify the government's role in fostering economic vitality, offering a spectrum of services to nurture new business ventures. Moreover, safety nets like unemployment benefits cultivate financial stability among citizens, translating into discretionary spending that fortifies businesses.

A mutually enriching exchange transpires in the unfolding dynamic between governments and businesses. Governments cultivate an environment that fuels business innovation and expansion through strategic maneuvers and visionary policy implementation. Businesses, in turn, become engines of growth and agents of economic transformation, amplifying the symphony of prosperity. As this harmonious interplay continues, economies evolve, elevating the quality of life and shaping the destiny of nations.

Encouraging Financial Inclusion

To be financially included means that all individuals and enterprises can access and effectively use various financial services. Services such as banking, investing, credit, and insurance fall under this category. The benefits of financial inclusion to both individuals and organizations are substantial. Financial institutions have only sometimes been good to those at the bottom of the economic ladder, including low-income people, women, and others on the margins of society. They have frequently relied on informal, unregulated financial tools because they need access to formal services and the freedom and ability to use them. This makes it more difficult for people and enterprises to take advantage of economic opportunities and recover from setbacks like high medical bills or natural disasters brought on by climate change compared to those with access to official services. A growing amount of evidence demonstrates that financial inclusion contributes to poverty reduction, crisis resilience, and other indicators of human progress.

The "financial inclusion" concept gained prominence during the early 2000s, although its origins can be linked to the microcredit movement that emerged in the 1970s. In recent times, it has risen in significance as a catalyst for worldwide development initiatives spanning fields like agriculture, education, and humanitarian assistance. It has become a mainstream objective of many international standard-setting agencies and national governments to attain policy goals outside the financial sector.

Many international organizations that provide money for development want to do the same. The CGAP Funder Survey found that $58 billion would be allocated for financial inclusion in 2020. While public sector organizations focus on traditional methods of addressing marginalized populations, private sector organizations ranging from huge incumbent financial institutions to fintech startups are investigating new, typically digital, approaches. The goal of financial inclusion for all has seen significant progress over the years. However, 1.4 billion adults still need access to the formal financial sector, and women still need to catch up to men in account ownership. In addition to filling these gaps, addressing the considerable risks provided by the innovations underpinning recent breakthroughs, such as risks to consumers' data protection and privacy, is essential to "deepen" the impact of financial services.

Providing access to financial services for people and businesses of all income levels will help alleviate poverty and income disparity. People can better manage their finances and increase their earning potential if they have financing, savings accounts, and financial literacy programs.

In particular, digital banking and mobile money have completely altered financial services distribution in emerging countries. Together, governments and financial firms can foster an environment where financial services can thrive and help more people gain access to them. Today, the concept of financial inclusion is crucial in the fight against poverty and income disparity. When people and businesses of all income levels and backgrounds can gain access to a full suite of financial products and services and products at reasonable prices, we have achieved financial inclusion.

Access to banking services allows people to better plan for the future by saving money and investing. By expanding access to banking and other financial services, financial inclusion helps to alleviate poverty and boost economic mobility. Access to credit is a key component of financial inclusion's ability to alleviate poverty. Credit makes it easier for people to launch and grow businesses, acquire property like a car or home, and further their education and professional development. With credit, people may be able to settle for low-paying employment they can afford.

Saving money and amassing riches are two additional benefits of being financially included. People with access to savings accounts can better prepare for the unexpected, cover large expenses, and save for the future. This can put them in a better position financially and help them avoid debt. Financial inclusion is effective in lowering income disparities. It is much easier for people to further their education, launch their enterprises, and increase their income when they have access to banking and other financial services. Income inequality and economic mobility may both improve as a result. There is a multiplicative effect of financial inclusion's advantages for society. Organizations with access to capital can grow their operations, boosting employment and the economy. New firms and industries may spring up due to expanding access to financial services.

Many people and enterprises need access to financial services despite the many advantages of financial inclusion. The World Bank estimates that 1.7% of the world's adult population has no bank account. This is a major constraint on the spread of banking services and the economy's expansion. Governments and financial organizations should collaborate to improve access to financial services and broaden financial inclusion. Investment in financial infrastructure, the creation of regulations that encourage financial inclusion, and public education about the value of financial services all fall under this category.

Governments and financial organizations can use technology to help more people access the financial system. Digital banking and mobile money have completely altered the banking and money transfer industries. Smartphones and mobile apps have made various financial services available to individuals at their convenience. Mobile money has been especially effective in expanding access to banking services in low-income regions.

There are currently more than a billion mobile money accounts in the world, per the World Bank. This has aided the cause of financial inclusion by making savings accounts, money transfers, and bill payments available to more people. Promoting financial literacy initiatives presents an additional avenue for achieving the objective of expanding access to financial services. A prevalent deficiency in financial literacy is observed among the general populace. A person's ability to manage money, save for the future, and invest in themselves can all be improved via participation in a financial literacy program.

Banks and other financial institutions should also do their part to advance this goal. They can collaborate on creating new financial services and products tailored to the requirements of those with lower incomes. This consists of low-interest and no-minimum-balance savings accounts, microloans, and loans to small businesses. The concept of financial inclusion is crucial in the fight against poverty and income disparity.

Better financial management, savings, and future investment are all possible when people and businesses have access to financial services. This can potentially lessen economic inequality and bring about a more equitable society. Investment in financial infrastructure, the creation of inclusive laws, and public education about the value of financial services are ways governments and financial institutions can work together to advance the cause of financial inclusion.

CHAPTER FIVE
SUPPORTING EDUCATION, RESEARCH & DEVELOPMENT

Education is impacted by poverty, which is well-known. Only some people with formal education are desperately poor. However, most adults in poverty today do not have a formal education. Their offspring are likewise more prone to be left out. This is a terrible injustice because education profoundly affects poverty by making its persistence less likely.

Many people believe that education is the key to surviving in today's world and thriving in it. Because of this, getting a good education is widely seen as the best way out of poverty. Getting an education can break the cycle of poverty that affects individuals, families, and entire communities. A good education helps kids grow up with better social, emotional, mental, and linguistic abilities.

People who go to school learn a lot of useful information and typically learn more advanced skills than those who don't. They can put their newfound knowledge to work by getting better-paying jobs and generally bettering their life. Approximately 171 million people might be lifted out of extreme poverty if all pupils in low-income nations possessed basic reading abilities (but no other skills). The world's poverty rate might be reduced by more than half if all adults had completed secondary school. Because of this, ensuring access to high-quality education is one of the United Nations' Sustainable Development Goals.

Investing in people and ensuring they have the skills they need to thrive is crucial now more than ever because of how the world's economy has shifted due to technological progress and globalization. Recent predictions put the number of jobs at risk of being automated away by robots in the year 2030 at over 2 billion. If every child graduated primary school and could read, 171 million people would be lifted out of extreme poverty.

That amounts to a global decrease of 12%. The Education Commission estimates that implementing its recommendations for better education may cut absolute poverty in half. Acquiring an education increases an individual's income, with each year of schooling contributing to approximately a 10% growth in earnings. Moreover, investing an extra year in education generates a return of $5 in low-income countries and $2.5 in lower-middle-income nations for every $1 invested.

Education helps lessen economic disparities. The gap between the working poor and the working rich might be reduced by 39% if people from both socioeconomic groups had access to the same level of education. Education contributes to economic expansion. Between 1965 and 2010, the growth rates of East Asia and Sub-Saharan Africa were significantly different. If all children in low-income nations were educated, their GDP per capita would be over 70 percent higher in 2050. Long-term GDP in sub-Saharan Africa would increase by 16% if the average age at which people complete post-secondary education were raised by one year. The planet can be saved through education.

By 2030, the effects of climate change, a rise in natural disasters, and decreased agricultural output could potentially force up to 122 million individuals into poverty. It is crucial to emphasize the significance of highly skilled and well-educated individuals in driving the growth of sustainable industries. One-third of all GHG emissions are caused by agriculture. Future farmers can benefit greatly from learning about agricultural sustainability issues in elementary and high school.

One of the most effective means of alleviating poverty on a global scale is to invest in areas such as education and R&D. More individuals will have the chance to acquire new knowledge and develop useful innovations if we help expand access to education and fund research. Education is crucial to increased financial security because it equips people with the knowledge and skills valued by employers. If we put money into education, more individuals will have access to the tools they need to start businesses and grow the economy.

The economy benefits greatly from research and development efforts as well. Businesses are motivated to invest in R&D when governments provide financial incentives, and the resulting innovations benefit consumers and businesses worldwide. By investing in R&D, we're urging businesses to be creative in their pursuit of answers to the world's most pressing challenges. Governments can help alleviate poverty by enacting laws that promote economic equality, in addition to funding education and R&D. Ensuring universal access to healthcare and stable food supplies is a first step toward helping people lift themselves out of poverty.

In addition, measures that reduce tax liability and increase access to social services can help alleviate the stresses associated with low incomes, allowing individuals to redirect their efforts toward creating wealth and improving their economic circumstances. Governments can aid in the fight against global poverty by funding initiatives like education, R&D, and economic equality policies. Through our combined endeavors, individuals will have the opportunity to access the resources necessary for enhancing their own lives as well as the well-being of their communities.

Governments may ensure that their citizens have a fair chance at making it in life by guaranteeing access to quality education, research and development funding, and policies encouraging economic equality. We can improve the world by ensuring everyone has the same opportunities to escape poverty and provide for their family. We can make meaningful progress toward eliminating global poverty and bringing about a more wealthy future if we put our attention on education, research and development, and economic policy. We have a moral obligation to help people improve their circumstances so that they can provide for their families.

Addressing poverty and fostering a fairer society demands dedicating resources to education, research, and development and implementing policies that advance economic parity. This approach lays the foundation for individuals to attain improved opportunities for success and forge a more promising future for themselves and their communities. We can improve the world by ensuring everyone has the same opportunities to escape poverty and provide for their family. The best strategy to eliminate poverty and build a fairer world is investing in education, R&D, and laws encouraging economic equality. Governments may aid in alleviating global poverty and developing a more prosperous future by providing citizens with access to education, resources for innovation, the development of new products, and regulations that encourage economic equality.

Through collaborative efforts like these, we can guarantee that every individual can thrive and secure a more promising future for their dear ones. These endeavors will contribute to a fairer global landscape, enabling everyone to break free from poverty and create improved circumstances for themselves and their families. It is in our self-interest to work toward a world with less poverty and a brighter economic future. The world can be made more just and prosperous if we invest in education and R&D Governments may ensure that everyone benefits from economic growth by ensuring that everyone has access to education, tools for innovation and product development, and regulations that encourage economic equality.

Fostering Economic Growth Through Infrastructure Development

The dynamics of economic growth are intricately interwoven with the development of infrastructure. This foundational pillar not only shapes the physical landscape but also fuels financial prosperity and opens avenues for employment. Embracing the notion that investing in infrastructure is synonymous with investing in the future, societies around the globe are channeling resources into building and maintaining critical networks that underpin modern life.

At the core of this approach lies the recognition that injecting capital into infrastructure yields multi-faceted returns. An instrumental facet is the generation of employment opportunities through labor-intensive techniques employed during construction and maintenance. The ripple effects of this endeavor extend far beyond the immediate workforce, nurturing a self-sustaining ecosystem of economic growth. A salient facet in this process is the establishment of backward and forward linkages, ushering in a greater reliance on locally sourced resources, including labor and materials. This localized economic stimulus enriches communities, stimulating commerce and fostering self-reliance.

Central to this discourse is the quintessential role of infrastructure in daily existence. Transportation networks facilitate the seamless movement of people and goods, energy systems power industries and homes alike, water distribution ensures sustenance and communication networks form the bedrock of global connectivity. These components, collectively termed infrastructure, influence the economic trajectory, shaping the contours of growth and prosperity.

A staggering reality surfaces when one contemplates the magnitude of global infrastructure investments. The annual expenditure surpassing $2.5 trillion underscores nations' resolute commitment to fortifying their foundations for growth. Yet, this staggering sum pales in comparison to the anticipated trajectory of economic expansion. To maintain pace with burgeoning GDP growth, the scale of infrastructural investments is poised to ascend further. This augments the urgency for comprehensive initiatives that encompass federal, state, and municipal governments alike, collaborating to address the infrastructural imperatives of our era.

Delving deeper into the quantifiable impact, the McKinsey Global Institute sheds light on the intricate interplay between infrastructure and socioeconomic returns. An astounding revelation emerges: the social and economic return on infrastructure investment approximates 20%. Every dollar committed to infrastructural enhancement generates a sustained boost of 20 cents to the GDP. This statistical manifestation underscores the resounding truth that investments in infrastructure cultivate tangible assets and yield enduring financial dividends.

Yet, the translation of infrastructural investments into tangible public benefits requires meticulous planning and discernment. Governments entrusted with the onus of project selection encounter a multi-faceted challenge: the selection of projects that bear the most substantial yield for the public. The confluence of diverse factors, including economic viability, societal impact, and long-term sustainability, demands a judicious approach to project prioritization.

Crucially, the potential for reaping social and economic benefits hinges on the sustainable support of infrastructural endeavors. Sustainability emanates from the dual streams of revenue generation and government sponsorship. Successfully orchestrating an infrastructure project necessitates a delicate equilibrium wherein the project's financial viability either stems from generated profits or government-backed funds. A precarious juncture arises when government-led projects are financed through borrowing but need to engender adequate revenue or indirect economic gains to offset costs. The resultant burden exacts a toll on financial resources, dampening the anticipated benefits and limiting the transformative potential.

Navigating the complex interplay of infrastructure development, economic growth, and societal advancement underscores the paramount importance of achieving a delicate balance. This equilibrium hinges on foresight, discerning investments, and a comprehensive approach to project selection and execution. The symphony of progress encompasses more than mere physical structures; it resonates with future generations' aspirations and potential. This harmonious composition blends the pragmatic considerations of infrastructure with the harmonious promises of prosperity, ensuring that the foundation of growth stands unwavering, fortified by today's investments for tomorrow's gains.

Methodology For Enhancing Infrastructure Decision-Making

The key best practices included in the framework aim to improve the social and economic impact of infrastructure decisions and bring them into the modern era. Each phase facilitates and contributes to a reliable, data-driven procedure for selecting and carrying out infrastructure projects. Making sure projects produce useful results is the starting point from which everything flows.

Creating Initiatives With Measurable Outcomes

Political considerations frequently influence the selection of infrastructure projects by governments. For instance, a national government may prioritize capital investment in a new port even if the project has a weak economic rationale because it would provide an easier point for trade with a politically aligned country. Another example would be a government spending money to build a new road in an electorally significant area to relieve traffic congestion there. Investments must generate clear economic and public benefits and build a competitive advantage. Still, in the current environment, countries, states, and cities must compete for trade, corporate headquarters, jobs, and talent, so government and citizens must be vigilant.

The selection of government projects should be based on trustworthy data and analytics, sound financial models, and citizen-centric designs to accomplish this. They need to think about how an infrastructure project will affect the world immediately and later. The following are examples of such consequences:

The elimination of economic bottlenecks leads to increased economic activity, which, in turn, catalyzes growth in labor and industrial productivity. The ripple effects of this progress encompass various facets, such as the infusion of wages into the local economy, the expansion of growth opportunities for local suppliers and contractors, and the amplification of multiplier effects. Furthermore, projects yield direct and indirect fiscal benefits for government budgets. These encompass direct taxes or fees collected from a project, like tolls, and indirect taxes or fees arising from the project's impact, exemplified by increased property taxes in areas where infrastructure, such as roads, is developed.

The transformative influence of projects extends beyond finances. It encompasses the growth of a region's talent pool, rendering it a more appealing place to reside. This, in turn, contributes to a larger tax base and heightened economic competitiveness. Additionally, improvements in the quality of life for residents manifest, as evidenced by reduced road congestion and enhanced accessibility. The "Rail plus Property" approach adopted by the Hong Kong Mass Transit Railway is an illustrative model of this symbiotic relationship between infrastructure and real estate.

The dismantling of economic barriers leads to a domino effect of positive outcomes. It generates a surge in economic activity, cultivates local businesses, bolsters fiscal revenues for governments, nurtures talent growth, enhances overall competitiveness, and augments the well-being of residents. This holistic impact underscores the interconnected nature of infrastructure and economic development, creating a cycle of progress that benefits society at large.

The objective is to set up a steady stream of high-quality initiatives in a standardized, repeatable fashion that can be measured for their positive impact on society and the economy. The case of Chile illustrates this method. The National Investment System at the Ministry of Housing and Urban Planning evaluates all proposed infrastructure projects using uniform templates, processes, and metrics. This committee, which rejects approximately 25 to 35 percent of requests, employs objective criteria that encompass factors such as the direct and indirect economic implications, as well as social aspects like the cost of travel time.

The Ministry of Finance makes the final call on projects and allocates funds based on a mix of cost-benefit analysis and national priorities. All metrics and performance data from previous iterations of a project are made publicly available in the interest of full disclosure. Make Better Use of Network Effects to Coordinate Infrastructure Investments. When deciding which projects to pursue, it's also crucial to consider the network impacts the investments will have on other parts of the system, especially when those parts are interconnected networks like transportation systems or electrical grids.

For instance, domestic travelers will not profit from network effects if a country has one commercial airport. However, if more airports are constructed, the benefits of the network as a whole will increase. According to studies, when added to an already existing but immature network, the marginal value of investing in infrastructure is the largest in developing nations. Adding to a mature network may not be as beneficial as investing in expanding a younger network with fewer nodes.

To take these network effects into account, governments should make decisions on a portfolio level, assessing initiatives in the context of the whole system rather than individually. Metro Atlanta, in the U.S. state of Georgia, considered numerous "debottlenecking" solutions by comparing portfolios with varying asset mixes. Each government project portfolio's overall performance impact and cost-benefit ratio were evaluated. Lack of cooperation between multiple regional agencies or levels of government is one barrier governments confront when attempting to perform such analyses.

Because of economies of scale in networks, which may go unnoticed by local decision-makers, proper coordination is crucial to reap the full benefits of these systems at the regional and national levels. Several approaches can improve coordination between different levels of government to lessen the impact of these difficulties. Interdepartmental committees and programs, for instance, can help break down bureaucratic barriers to coordination. Strategic frameworks for infrastructure investment can be used to facilitate the alignment of goals across agencies and jurisdictions.

To take things to the next level, governments may create a national infrastructure bank to fund projects directly, coordinate investments among regional institutions, and act as a repository for information. A national coordinating entity like a bank like this would make it easier to choose projects with the portfolio as a whole in mind. Involve and coordinate community members to expand access to economic and social benefits. Governments should consider social equality when making infrastructure expenditures to ensure that the potential economic advantages accrue to all citizens. Whether investments benefit people of different ages, incomes, locations (urban vs. rural), races, and ethnicities is an important question to ask. More weight is generally given to projects that benefit those who could benefit the most economically.

Governments are more likely to evaluate the full implications of an investment if they convey a complete understanding of the impact. Engaging the public, the commercial sector, and civil society players in infrastructure design and implementation is crucial to guaranteeing more inclusive benefits. Consultations allow governments to tell the public about possible projects (including the findings of economic, environmental, and social impact assessments) and receive feedback from the general populace. That will raise the chance of equitable outcomes and increase public satisfaction with the chosen infrastructure projects.

Get Access To Long-Term Funding

As we've seen, the community and economy benefit from infrastructure investments meeting identified requirements. Since infrastructure projects often have multiyear planning and construction timeframes, and adoption and full usage of the assets might ramp up slowly, these benefits may not be realized for a long time. Nonetheless, infrastructure initiatives occasionally necessitate short- or intermediate-term borrowing, with conditions often tailored to market dynamics rather than the project's economic fundamentals. This discrepancy implies that even if significant infrastructure undertakings are completed within the stipulated timeframe and budget, governments are obligated to reimburse creditors for their expenses long before tangible economic advantages materialize. Governments can coordinate with long-term capital providers to schedule loan repayments to coincide with when the infrastructure's benefits will be fully realized. Fortunately, long-term money is readily available to invest in projects with a solid plan.

Investors have expanded their capital investment to infrastructure, making private cash more readily available. Since 2011, twice as many institutional investors have had a hand in infrastructure, and more than half intend to increase their long-term holdings in the sector. The top 10 public pension funds with infrastructure assets have had their holdings more than triple since 2011. Public pension funds intend to increase future allocations to infrastructure. Thus, these tendencies are likely to persist.

While there is a great demand and opportunity for infrastructure development, many long-term capital providers can only assume limited risks associated with new technology and new markets. Therefore, many developing market governments or those with bad credit ratings need help accessing long-term finance. These governments may look at novel models and solutions that reduce the risks of projects for long-term capital providers to get beyond these roadblocks. Development financing institutions and, increasingly, the private sector offer credit-support mechanisms such as political risk, demand, and stop-loss guarantees. Investments in sustainable infrastructure technology are prime candidates for such support mechanisms if a project provides benefits for the climate, as there is a growing readiness to underwrite risks that long-term capital sources may not accept.

Practices That Governments Can Use To Update And Enhance Their Infrastructure Decision-Making

For instance, up to a certain limit, IFC will guarantee payment in full and on time for debt service under its partial credit guarantee program. The administration of the Chuvash Republic utilized such a tool to attract private funding to improve the region's water supply, transportation, and housing. The government was able to get longer-term funding than it would have been able to secure without the IFC's guarantee of up to 23% of the principal on the government's bonds. To better align its debt with long-term infrastructure assets, Johannesburg, South Africa, used a partial credit guarantee to increase the credit on its municipal bonds by three notches, extending their duration from six to twelve years. Towards a uniform, data-driven approach to infrastructure decision-making

The features of our methodology include:

- A project's ability to provide substantial public benefits.
- Its compatibility with other projects.
- Its suitable alignment with community goals.
- It uses the best long-term funding options.

Therefore, governments may have to commit to transparent evaluations that contain the required checks and balances and invest in the capacity to do so. Governments should evaluate their infrastructure project development processes by mapping them against the aspects of the framework.

Can the government complete a formalized assessment of public benefits? Is there a way to evaluate the complete portfolio of the debt-management plan?

Governments can benefit from this evaluation by learning where they can enhance their operations by adopting new procedures, developing specific competencies, and disseminating relevant data. Building an entirely new governing system may be essential to properly choose and carry out infrastructure projects.

The Role of Foreign Aid in Ending Poverty

Poverty can be alleviated in several ways, one of which is with the help of foreign aid. Foreign aid is used to finance long-term projects that increase the quality of life in poor countries. This funding might improve access to education and healthcare and generate new employment possibilities for those who currently lack them. Food and medicine are two examples of essentials that can be provided by foreign aid and directly impact healthcare and the elimination of hunger. Access to new markets and investment possibilities are two ways foreign aid can stimulate economic expansion.

Many people in developing countries may be able to climb out of poverty if their economies see a boost from greater economic activity. It is crucial to have access to clean water, sanitation, and electricity, all of which can be improved with the support of foreign aid. Therefore, it is evident that aid from abroad can significantly impact the fight against global poverty. But if it is not spent wisely and effectively, this money will not help the poor long-term. Thus, governments from other countries must ensure that foreign aid funds go to projects and programs to help alleviate poverty. Foreign aid can be a powerful weapon in the war against poverty.

In addition, it is crucial to guard against the misuse of funds intended for international help. Unfortunately, this has been an issue in many nations, as unscrupulous officials have siphoned money from anti-poverty initiatives for their advantage. To avoid this, funds allocated for foreign help must be dispersed effectively and openly, with enough safeguards to prevent misuse.

By focusing on these areas, foreign aid can become a potent instrument in the fight against global poverty. Foreign aid is a crucial component of the solution if countries are serious about alleviating global poverty. Foreign aid can make a significant difference in the fight against global poverty if it is invested in long-term projects that raise living standards and expand prospects for sustainable economic growth. If we want to end poverty for good, it's up to all nations to coordinate their efforts to maximize the impact of foreign aid.

The United States contributed $35.5 billion to international aid in 2020, making it the top donor in the world. These numbers are from the Organization for Economic Cooperation and Development. Foreign aid is sent to developing nations for disaster prevention, disaster relief, economic growth, and poverty alleviation efforts. The United States Agency for International Development (USAID) is the principal agency among the 20 U.S. government entities overseeing such initiatives. Together, USAID and its partners teach individuals to become more self-sufficient.

USAID's strategy emphasizes free and open, enterprise-driven development to create robust market economies in which state sovereignty and individual dignity and rights are respected. The agency noted that this bolsters the efforts of partner countries to improve their governance, institutions, laws, and structures as valued participants in the international community and global economy. U.S. foreign aid starkly contrasts governments that provide loans at exorbitant interest rates, making it difficult for debtor nations to repay. That can put undue stress on communities and nations already struggling under the weight of debt. Governments that provide these loans often also bring in their citizens to work on development projects in the countries that receive them.

Foreign aid has been proven effective time and time again throughout history. The United Nations Millennium Development Goals were an ambitious framework for governments, nonprofit organizations, and businesses in the private sector to use to reduce poverty. These goals successfully did what they set out:

- Decrease global poverty and mortality rates from preventable diseases.
- Increase educational enrollment.
- Increase environmental sustainability.
- Promote gender equality.

The under-five mortality rate, the number of persons living in extreme poverty, and the proportion of children of school age who were not in school all dropped by about half between 1990 and 2015. Only approximately 22.5 percent of U.S. foreign aid goes directly to governments; the rest is redistributed to NGOs, NGOs, and private enterprises so that they can do the work best suited to them. Only countries that adhere to the Millennium Challenge Account's rigorous accountability and transparency standards are eligible to receive direct government support. Therefore, it is less likely that many believe foreign aid will end up in corrupt governments.

Allocating foreign aid only for the benefit of its beneficiaries would be a worthwhile use of U.S. resources. Still, it would also be self-serving, as it would help the U.S. achieve its goals of promoting democracy and economic growth around the world. This is why the goals of both foreign aid and military spending are frequently the same, yet how they are pursued is frequently at odds with one another. Opting for peaceful economic and humanitarian assistance whenever feasible is a more favorable approach than resorting to perilous and aggressive military actions.

U.S. Senators Murphy and Van Hollen, along with Representatives Cicilline and Bera, have introduced a budget amendment called "Investing in 21st Century Diplomacy," which states that "it shouldn't have taken 500,000 dead Americans to illustrate that our principal dangers are non-military in character." This also brings up the notion that global threats like climate change and illness can be fought through international aid rather than the military. When it comes to strengthening national security, foreign aid is crucial because it lessens the need for costly and perhaps lethal military deployments. Political unrest and extremism are sometimes fostered by economic instability.

Spreading foreign aid proactively and strategically could reduce political unrest. For every $1 invested in conflict prevention, we save $16 in response costs and avoid sending our troops into harm's way, as stated in a letter to House and Senate leaders from numerous high-ranking military officers. The United States also benefits from the economic growth fostered by foreign aid. Reducing extreme poverty allows people to become consumers of U.S. goods and services, the vast majority of whom are located outside of the United States. U.S. companies see huge returns on tiny investments in the impoverished world. U.S. exports from newly industrialized countries like South Korea, Brazil, and Mexico have historically generated returns on assistance investments.

CHAPTER SIX

MEASURING THE IMPACT OF WEALTH CREATION STRATEGIES

The term "wealth" refers to the total monetary value of a person, group, organization, or nation. The formula for calculating wealth is the market value of all tangible and intangible assets, less liabilities. Accumulating a large number of rare items is the essence of wealth. Individuals, businesses, or countries are considered wealthy when they amass a lot of money and other assets. Wealth can be viewed in absolute or relative terms and compared with income, which can be considered flows.

The "wealth effect" hypothesizes that when widely held assets, such as real estate and equities, increase in value, people are more likely to increase their discretionary spending. It stands to reason that an increase in one's wealth would encourage more spending by that individual. A homeowner or 401(k) participant sitting on significant profits might be tempted to buy a new flat-screen television or sport utility vehicle. Some analysts disagree, arguing that while real estate appreciation does lead to an increase in wealth, stock market appreciation does not. Investors should be wary of the wealth effect regardless of its source (real estate or the stock market), as spending unrealized gains vulnerable to reversal is rarely wise.

Financial Literacy

There are many manifestations of affluence. In a strict material sense, one's wealth is the total of all tangible assets. In the financial world, one's net worth is the most prevalent measure of success. Historically, societies' definitions and measurements of wealth have varied. Money is the standard unit of measurement for success in today's economy. Money's function as a unit of account is exemplified by its use to measure wealth. This method of evaluating wealth is susceptible to large swings due to the ability of outside forces to alter the value of money. Still, it does serve as a useful benchmark nonetheless. Without other indicators of wealth, land and livestock can serve as surrogates. For instance, the ancient Egyptians used wheat as a proxy for prosperity. Sheep, horses, and cattle are common forms of currency in herding societies.

The difficulty of assessing wealth in the form of many items can be circumvented by measuring wealth in monetary terms. It is then possible to perform arithmetic operations on these numbers. Consequently, this makes it possible to use net worth instead of wealth per se—assets minus debts equal net value. In the context of a company, net worth is synonymous with shareholders' equity or book value. When describing an individual, net worth represents a gauge of their wealth, encompassing all assets and holdings under their ownership and control while subtracting any existing debts or liabilities.

Money comes in the form of a flow, while wealth stays put. Wealth is the stockpile of valuable economic items at a certain time, while income is the sum of money or products earned over a period. Money earned is added to one's fortune (or subtraction, if negative). Over time, a person with a positive net income will amass more and more wealth. Gross domestic product (GDP) is sometimes incorrectly interpreted as a measure of a country's wealth, whereas it is a measure of income (a flow variable) (a stock variable). Although "rich" is often used in a relative sense, it can be used by anyone who has gained substantial wealth. Total wealth might differ for different people, whether counted in dollars and cents or wheat and sheep. Who is considered wealthy and who is not is typically determined by comparing individuals' levels of wealth to those of other groups.

Repeated studies have found that individuals' estimations of their wealth relative to others significantly impact their perceptions of their well-being and happiness rather than absolute riches. Items that are plentiful and free for all offer no basis for relative comparisons between people, which is why the term wealth is typically only applied to scarce economic goods.

A nation's wealth can be broken down for simplicity. The term "produced capital" refers to the wide range of manmade assets in the economy, including but not limited to transportation networks, ports, buildings, and machines. Wood, minerals, oil, and gas are all examples of natural capital. It also encompasses several habitats, such as wetlands, which filter water for human consumption, and forests, which sequester carbon. Human capital is the sum of a population's formal and informal educational experiences and resulting workplace knowledge, skills, and talents. Stocks, bonds, and other financial assets are all considered part of "financial capital." Stocks of manufactured and monetary capital are frequently the target of government, business, and individual investments.

The behaviors and values that form social capital include people's feelings of safety in their communities, openness to accepting others, and trust in institutions. These aspects, along with the five elements of a comprehensive wealth portfolio, play a role in society's broader concept of well-being. Whether a country's overall wealth is growing over time holds significant importance. If it is, the nation is likely experiencing long-term progress and a continuous or increasing level of prosperity. On the other hand, if wealth isn't increasing, progress will halt, leading to a decline in living standards. Because of this, measuring total wealth is gaining recognition as an increasingly crucial factor in monitoring societal development.

Developing Performance Indicators

Performance Indicators are metrics used to monitor and analyze key aspects of your operations. The performance indicators you track can tell you a lot about how well your company is doing. Your Performance Indicators can help you identify problems and take corrective action before you incur significant losses. The performance indicator quantification then lets you evaluate your results. As a result, your company's operational model will be more secure over time, and its investment value will rise.

Your company's first order of business is to recognize and comprehend the significance of the numerous financial realities reflected in your P.I. data. Leverage the insights obtained from these vital indicators of financial management performance to identify and rectify any concerns stemming from policies, processes, staff, or products that might adversely impact your core performance metrics. These key performance indicators can be utilized to evaluate the effectiveness of your asset management:

Mean Time to Failure (MTTF)

Mean time to failure (MTTF) This criterion is typically used for consumables, such as light bulbs, that cannot be repaired and must be replaced. Its purpose is to verify that the installed assets are performing as expected. It could also mean the provider needs to be more high-quality or have adequate storage conditions. Using light bulbs as an example, if 50% of the supply fails 50% earlier than projected by MTTF calculations, this could indicate a quality control fault on the manufacturer's part. This formula can determine MTTF: Total assets in use / Total operational hours.

Annualized Failure Rate (AFR)

Annualized failure rate (AFR) Technology businesses frequently utilize this statistic, which provides a rate rather than an average, to spot performance concerns. A high AFR may affect a company's performance, like in the case of a hard disk drive manufacturing plant. They looked into the matter and found that it was due to a flaw in quality control. As a result of their process improvements, their AFR has decreased significantly. An approximation of the AFR formula is hours per year recorded / meantime recorded between failures.

Mean Time to Repair (MTTR)

Average repair duration measures how long it takes to fix a given asset. This key performance indicator can be utilized to gain insight into the asset or the maintenance procedure. When the time required to fix a product grows noticeably compared to its past performance, it may be time to consider a replacement. If maintenance teams lack the necessary tools or expertise, it may be a sign that the company needs to reevaluate its approach to personnel or inventory management. To determine MTTR, use the following formula: Maintenance time/number of repairs.

Mean time between failures (MTBF)

The mean time between failure (MTBF) estimates how long an asset will last before breaking down. Analysts might use failure probability to inform business decisions like upping maintenance spending. A product's breakdown could lead to a bigger issue, but frequent maintenance could keep that from happening. If, on the other hand, MTBF rates are low, the organization may want to look into whether or not it is performing maintenance that isn't necessary. Using the formula Time in Service / Number of Breakdowns, calculate MTBF.

Days Sales Of Inventory (DSI)

These metric measures the days it would take to sell the entire stock. In simpler terms, it indicates how quickly the stock is being turned over, and accumulating unsold products wastes money and valuable warehouse space. Monitoring daily stock sales helps the purchasing manager understand consumer buying patterns and make informed purchase decisions. When you combine the formula for average inventory with this metric, you get DSI (Days Sales of Inventory).

It can be calculated as (Average Inventory / COGS) x 365

Overall Equipment Effectiveness (OEE)

The efficiency of pie-making machinery over a specific timeframe is gauged using its Overall Equipment Efficiency (OEE). This metric is the benchmark for assessing various manufacturing indicators due to its capacity to uncover inefficiencies, assess progress, and enhance machinery productivity. A flawless score suggests that the machinery is defect-free and the factory is running at its maximum potential. The formula for calculating OEE can be simplified as follows:

OEE is calculated as performance x availability x quality

Inventory Turnover Ratio (ITR)

A company's inventory turnover ratio measures how often its stock has been depleted and replenished. How efficiently a business turns its inventory into cash is evaluated. Strong sales are indicative of a ratio that is higher than 1. Hence, a larger ratio is preferable. To begin, determine the typical stock: The typical stock level is calculated as follows:

ITR = sales price / typical stock on hand

Average Occupancy Rate (AOR)

The occupancy rate of a building is the ratio of the number of occupied units to the total number of available units during a given time frame. A higher occupancy rate means more money in the bank for the asset manager. Management still has to cover utilities for empty rooms. Thus, they generate no income at all. Staffing, stock levels, and service availability can also be figured out with the help of the AOR. Hotel management, for instance, would know that summer is peak season because AOR often rises during that time. Here is the formula for determining AOR: total number of rooms already occupied / total number of rooms yet to be occupied.

On-Time Delivery (OTD) Rate

On-time delivery (OTD) rate, although most commonly associated with tangible goods, can also stand for the timely distribution of an electronic file. This metric can be used to detect problems with the quality of service provided to customers or to track out sources of waste in the supply chain. A low OTD could be due to technical difficulties, scheduling constraints, or a need for more personnel when dealing with digital products. This formula can be used to determine OTD:

On-time delivery = (total number of deliveries - delayed deliveries) / total number of deliveries

Utilizing Data and Analytics to Track Progress

The necessity to track and assess KPIs is something that every organization must face. The larger the corporation, the more complex the issue, as different divisions, businesses, and departments will have different goals and approaches. Strong enterprise data governance is essential because of the importance of data management. To illustrate, let's imagine you're interested in finding the answer to the seemingly straightforward question, "Who are my most profitable customers?" To do this, you'll need access to customer information, product sales information, and marketing and sales expense data from across the company. Even if you succeed, it may be challenging to determine how much money is tied to a specific client. For instance, if your organization is multinational and complex, you must verify that your sales teams have correctly identified the operations for which they have invoiced purchases. It's easy to figure out that Shell PLC is the Parent Corporation of Shell USA and Shell UK, but what about Pennzoil and Jiffy Lube? They're a Shell company, too.

Reasons Good Data Governance Is Crucial

Data needed for analytics and profitability calculations are often dispersed among systems, adding further complexity. Is there only ever going to be one instance of the ERP software, even if it is the standard? What about segments of buyers, sellers, and purchases? Do you use a single, unified hierarchy for categorizing your data? What happens if you acquire a company that uses other software and has a different organizational structure, though?

The Benefits Of Data Governance

A set of practices known as "data governance" has been developed to actively manage and control data and its use within an organization. Creating internal data standards, norms, and enforcement mechanisms can assist in guaranteeing that information is reliable, consistent, and used appropriately. Here are some of a business's most important gains with good data governance.

Higher Productivity

Numerous effectiveness aspects can be improved by employing business analytics on carefully managed data. Through this, you can enhance the precision of your marketing and sales strategies by recognizing your most lucrative clientele. Generally, around 20% of your customer base tends to contribute to approximately 80% of your total revenue. Knowing the product's profitability allows you to cut losses on unprofitable lines while expanding your spending on successful ones. Opportunities for improvement in business processes can be uncovered through analysis, but only if the data used to inform such analyses can be trusted.

Enhanced Quality Of Data

Even with substantial investments in information technology, ensuring top-notch data quality remains a pressing issue. A staggering 95% of businesses experience the repercussions of inadequate data quality, which can even result in business failure. The consequences of subpar data quality translate to an average annual cost of $12.9 million for companies. Since data quality issues can have far-reaching consequences, improving them is essential to data governance initiatives. With better data quality, businesses and governments can reduce operational mistakes and boost the precision of their analyses. While there is no silver bullet, developing a data quality attitude and doing frequent audits and measurements of data quality as part of the governance process are important places to start.

Increased Conformity

There are severe consequences for noncompliance with regulations in healthcare, financial services, and other sectors. Pharmaceutical firms, for instance, are legally obligated to monitor their advertising and promotion costs. Since 2009, the United States Department of Justice has reached settlements totaling billions and hundreds of millions of dollars due to regulatory violations. This level of money necessitates meticulous record-keeping and auditability. Additional compliance requirements for using customer personal data in several domains are provided by the General Data Protection Regulation (GDPR), the California Customer Privacy Act (CalOPPA), and other data privacy regulations.

Companies risk penalties and litigation without robust data security and privacy policies supported by sound governance.

Improved Ability To Make Choices

If your company has reliable information, it can make informed business judgments. Managers and employees can make better decisions about marketing campaigns, price changes, product strategy, customer service, and other areas of the organization. However, this depends on users' access to reliable analytics, corporate intelligence, and strategic planning information.

Better Company

The advantages mentioned above should ultimately result in more money coming in. It appears that successful businesses place a greater emphasis on data governance than their competitors. For instance, "breakaway companies" were twice as likely to strongly agree in a 2018 McKinsey survey that their data governance strategy allowed them to identify and prioritize critical data assets. Any company-wide effort should boost operational efficiency; data governance is key to that process.

Improved Public Perception Of The Company

In addition to the bottom line, good data governance can improve how customers feel about a company. For instance, better interactions between sales and customer service agents and customers are made possible by high-quality data. As a result, customers will be happier and more loyal to the company, which should lead to even more growth.

Data Governance: How to Create a Plan

While I.T. departments were often assumed to be responsible for data governance, it is now widely understood that they need to possess the power necessary to establish and consistently apply enterprise-wide data standards. Such activities must be driven by business management, and a data governance program will often have a steering committee comprised of top executives and other data owners to guarantee this happens. It should also settle disagreements over the "proper" data definition or classification, with the power to require departments to adjust their systems and procedures to meet the prescribed standard. Data stewards, typically data-savvy business users from across the firm, are tasked with monitoring data sets, enforcing data standards part-time, and supporting the steering committee. The average business has four full-time data governance employees and nine part-time data stewards.

How can you acquire the desired results and reap the benefits of an efficient data governance endeavor once the governance framework has been established? To compile The Information Difference benchmark database, a thorough survey is taken by the companies who participate. Response data analysis reveals striking differences in practice between firms that evaluate themselves highly and those that do not work in data governance.

The following are characteristics of effective data governance programs. Data models for important business data domains, policies to limit access to sensitive or essential data, a clear process for resolving disputes, extensive documenting of business processes, regular data quality audits, and a risk register highlighting data-related business hazards. Such initiatives also feature data governance education and a method for sharing program outcomes. The data governance benefits your company anticipates are within reach, and you may get there by following the procedures detailed here.

Gross Domestic Profit

The total monetary or market worth of all final goods and services produced inside a country's boundaries over a given period is known as the country's gross domestic product (GDP). The GDP is a barometer of a country's economic health because it measures its total output. Gross domestic product is normally computed once per year, but quarterly estimates are often available. For instance, the government produces an annualized GDP estimate each fiscal quarter and annually in the United States. All the data presented in this report has been adjusted for inflation to make the current values meaningful.

What You Need to Know (GDP)

Gross domestic product (GDP) includes all final goods and services purchased and produced within a country and all final goods and services produced abroad. The value is increased by exports and decreased by imports. The foreign trade balance is one of the most crucial parts of a country's gross domestic product. For a country's GDP to rise, exports must be worth more than imports. A trade surplus happens when a country's exports exceed its imports.

Conversely, a trade deficit develops when domestic consumer spending on foreign goods exceeds the quantity domestic producers can sell overseas consumers. The country's GDP usually falls when this happens. A nominal and a real GDP can be calculated, with the latter considering inflation. Since real GDP employs constant dollars, it is a more accurate measure of a country's economic health across time. Imagine a country in 2012 with a nominal GDP of $100 billion. Its nominal GDP will reach $150 billion by 2022. In the same time frame, price increases averaged 100%. If one were to base their assessment of the country's economic health on its nominal GDP, one might conclude that it is doing quite well. However, a reduction in real economic performance over this time is revealed by the fact that the real GDP (expressed in 2012 dollars) would only be $75 billion.

There are multiple approaches to presenting GDP, each providing a slightly distinct perspective.

Nominal Gross Domestic Product

Calculating an economy's output at current prices is its nominal GDP. That is to say, it doesn't adjust for factors like inflation or growing price levels, which might artificially boost the growth rate. All products and services included in the calculation of nominal GDP are evaluated at their market prices in the given year. To make direct economic comparisons between countries, the nominal GDP is calculated in either the native currency or U.S. dollars based on market exchange rates. GDP is nominal when comparing quarterly results within the same year. GDP from multiple years can be compared by using real GDP. This is because volume comparisons across years are more meaningful when inflation is taken into account less frequently.

GDP in Constant Prices

To isolate the effect of inflation or deflation on the trend in output over time, real GDP is a measure of economic output that accounts for price stability from one year to the next. Inflation can affect GDP since it relies on the dollar value of production. A country's GDP usually goes up when prices go up, but that doesn't mean that production has increased or improved. Therefore, it might be hard to identify whether an increase in an economy's GDP was due to a real production expansion or just rising prices if only the nominal GDP exists. Economists calculate real GDP by adjusting for inflation. Economists can account for inflation by comparing the current year's output to the output of a reference year, known as the base year. This allows us to see whether a country is growing by comparing GDP from year to year.

A GDP price deflator, the price change between the current and base years, is used to derive real GDP. The deflator would be 1.05 if prices increased by 5% from the base year. Real GDP is derived by dividing nominal GDP by this deflator. Inflation usually is positive, making nominal GDP greater than actual GDP. When comparing output numbers from one year to the next, real GDP helps smooth out fluctuations in market value. A significant gap between a country's real GDP and nominal GDP may signal high levels of inflation or deflation.

Calculating GDP on an Individual Basis

Assessing a nation's living standards often involves using gross domestic product (GDP) per capita. This measure suggests that a country's overall quality of life can be deduced from its per capita output or income. There are distinct measurements for gross domestic product per individual, including nominal, real (adjusted for inflation), and purchasing power parity (PPP) assessments.

Per capita gross domestic product, in the simplest terms, measures the share of a country's total economic output that can be credited to each of its citizens. Since GDP market value per person can be used as a measure of affluence, this can be used as a proxy for a country's overall wealth. It is common practice to compare GDP per capita to the more common GDP measures. Economists rely on this measure to better understand national and international productivity. The GDP per capita considers a country's GDP and population.

For this reason, it may be instructive to disentangle the various influences on GDP growth per person. For example, suppose a country's per-capita GDP rises while its population stays unchanged. This may be due to technological advances that allow for greater output using the same labor force. Suppose a country has a high GDP per person but a low total population. In that case, it has likely developed a robust, resource-based economy that allows it to function independently.

Economic Output Rate

To determine how quickly an economy is expanding, analysts examine the percentage increase or decrease in GDP from one year (or quarter) to the next. Because GDP growth is widely believed to be strongly related to key policy aims like inflation and unemployment rates, it is a popular metric among economic policymakers, who typically represent it as a percentage. A rapid increase in GDP growth could indicate that the economy is heating up, prompting the Fed to consider raising interest rates. In contrast, a slowing or negative GDP growth rate (a recession) is interpreted by central banks as a signal that interest rates need to be cut and stimulus may be required.

Comparative of GDP and PPP

Although not a direct measure of GDP, purchasing power parity (PPP) is employed by economists to facilitate comparisons between countries in terms of real output, real income, and living standards. This is achieved by accounting for variations in local prices and the cost of living.

GDP Modeling

GDP can be computed using three primary methods, each of which, when accurately executed, should yield the same overall value. These three methodologies are commonly referred to as the "expenditure approach," the "output approach," and the "income approach."

Spending Methodology

The expenditure method, also known as the spending method, determines how much money is being spent by various sectors of the economy. When calculating GDP in the United States, the spending method is used most frequently. The formula for this method is as follows:

GDP = Consumption + Government + spending + Investment = Net exports

All these activities contribute to a country's GDP. When you "consume" something, you spend money on things for your use. This spending on items like food and haircuts adds up. In the United States, over two-thirds of the GDP comes from consumer spending. Consequently, consumer confidence plays a crucial role in the GDP expansion. How willing consumers are to spend money reflects their confidence levels. Low confidence signals concerns about the future and a careful approach to significant purchases.

Additionally, government spending encompasses both direct and indirect expenses. Equipment, infrastructure, and salaries are all areas where governments must spend money. Government spending may become increasingly important as a percentage of GDP when consumer and business investments fall. Private domestic investment or capital expenditures are what is meant by the term "investment." To advance their operations, businesses must occasionally fork up cash. For instance, a company may invest in new machinery. Business investment is essential to GDP since it raises a country's productive capacity and creates new jobs.

To calculate net exports (N.X.), subtract total exports from total imports. Net exports are the products and services produced within a country that are sold abroad, less the value of imports purchased by domestic customers—companies' total spending in a country, whether domestic or foreign, is factored into the total.

Methods Based On Output Production

Compared to the expenditure strategy, the production approach is the exact opposite. The production approach calculates the value of the economy's output by estimating its final product and subtracting the value of the intermediate items used in its creation (like those of materials and services). The production approach takes a retrospective view from the endpoint of economic activity, while the spending approach forecasts future costs.

The Money Method

The income method is a compromise between the other two methods of GDP calculation. The income method totals the earnings of all economic players, including laborers' pay, landowners' rent, investors' interest income, and businesses' net revenue. Some modifications are included in the income method for things that aren't technically wages paid to workers. For example, Sales and property taxes are examples of indirect business taxes. In addition, firms also contribute a reserve known as depreciation to the GDP to cover the cost of replacing equipment that wears out over time. All of these things add up equal to a country's GDP.

What Is the Difference Between GDP, GNP, and GNI?

While widely used, GDP is not the sole gauge of a nation's economic well-being. Gross domestic product (GDP) evaluates the country's production of businesses and individuals. In contrast, gross national product (GNP) encompasses the output of both domestically established and foreign-owned businesses and individuals. In contrast, the gross national product (GNP) accounts for the output of all domestically based and foreign-owned businesses and individuals. Exports by other countries are not counted toward GNP. Growth can also be quantified by the country's gross national income (GNI). The GDP is the total money a country's residents earn yearly (regardless of whether the underlying economic activity occurs domestically or abroad). Similar to how the income approach to calculating GDP is related to the production (output) approach, so is the relationship between GNP and GNI.

The GDP uses a production-based methodology, while the GNI is based on income. Using GNI, a nation's wealth is evaluated by adding its GDP to its indirect taxation and depreciation on business activity (as well as its net foreign factor income). The net foreign factor income is arrived at by deducting the whole amount paid to foreign firms and persons from the total amount paid to domestic firms. It has been argued that GNI, rather than GDP, maybe a more appropriate indicator of the state of the economy in today's interconnected world. The GDP of certain countries is significantly higher than their GNI since most of their money is sent outside by foreign firms and people.

For instance, consider the case of Luxembourg. In 2019, the small European nation of Luxembourg displayed a significant contrast between its Gross Domestic Product (GDP) and Gross National Income (GNI). This discrepancy largely resulted from substantial payments rendered by foreign corporations that conducted business within Luxembourg, enticed by the country's advantageous tax policies. Contrarily, there is little to no difference between GNI and GDP in America—the U.S. As of the first quarter of 2023, GDP was $26.49 trillion, and GNI was $23.62 trillion at the end of 2021.

GDP readjustments

A country's GDP can be made more helpful by making several modifications. Economists can learn a lot about the size of a country's economy by looking at its GDP, but this number tells them very little about its average income or living conditions. This is partly because population density and standard of living vary considerably from one region to the next. Since China has around 300 times the population of Ireland, comparing the two countries' nominal GDPs tells us little about the realities of living in both countries. Statistical comparisons of GDP per capita between nations are occasionally used to shed light on this issue. The per capita gross domestic product (GDP), determined by dividing the total GDP by the population, is a commonly used measure of a nation's prosperity.

However, it should be noted that this metric has its limitations. To illustrate, let's imagine that China has a per capita GDP of $1,500, while Ireland's stands at $15,000. That doesn't mean Irish people are ten times better off than Chinese people on average. The cost of living is not factored into GDP per capita.

The Purchasing Power Parity (PPP) method addresses this issue by comparing the number of products and services that a given amount can buy in two nations after considering the difference in exchange rates. One of the most important indicators of prosperity is real per-capita GDP, calculated by adjusting GDP for buying power parity. A person's annual income in Ireland could be over $100,000, but in China, it could be under $50,000. The Irish worker comes out ahead in nominal terms. However, if the cost of living is three times higher in Ireland than in China, the Chinese worker will have a larger real income because of the higher purchasing power of the yuan.

Methods for Analyzing GDP

Most countries typically release monthly and quarterly GDP reports. The Bureau of Economic Analysis (BEA) in the United States issues a preliminary report on quarterly GDP four weeks after the end of each quarter and a more comprehensive report on quarterly GDP three months after the end of each quarter. Economists and investors alike can benefit from the amount of information provided by the BEA's comprehensive and detailed releases. Since GDP is a retrospective indicator and a prolonged period passes between the end of a quarter and its release, its effect on the market is typically muted. However, if the actual GDP numbers significantly diverge from forecasts, this information can affect the markets.

Businesses can use GDP as a reference for company strategy because it directly reflects the health and growth of the economy. Government agencies, like the Federal Reserve in the United States, factor in the GDP growth rate and other GDP statistics when deciding on monetary policy. An expansionary monetary policy may be adopted if the growth rate decelerates. Monetary policy could slow the economy if the growth rate is strong to prevent inflation.

GDP and Expenditures

Investors closely monitor GDP since it is a basis for making business decisions. If you're an equity investor, you'll want to check out the pre-tax profits, operating cash flows, and sector breakdowns shown in the GDP report's corporate earnings section. The inventory data is also useful. The asset allocation process can benefit from comparing GDP growth rates across countries, providing more informed choices regarding whether or not to invest in countries with rapidly expanding economies.

The total market capitalization to GDP ratio, expressed as a percentage, serves as a valuable metric that investors can utilize to gauge the valuation of a stock market. Comparing a company's market capitalization to its total sales (or revenues) is the closest thing to this regarding stock valuation, and the resulting ratio is the familiar price-to-sales ratio. Market capitalization as a percentage of GDP varies substantially between countries, just as the price-to-sales ratio of stocks in different industries varies widely. According to data from the World Bank, the market capitalization relative to gross domestic product stood at 195% in the United States in 2020, 83% in China, and an astonishing 1,777% in Hong Kong.

However, this ratio becomes useful compared to the norms established over time in a specific country. FOR INSTANCE, the U.S.'s market capitalization to gross domestic product ratio fell from 142% at the end of 2006 to 79% by the end of 2008. These, looking back, were the extremes of overvaluation and undervaluation for American stocks. Investors only receive an update once every quarter, and adjustments can be high enough to significantly alter the percentage change in GDP, which is the largest drawback of using this data.

Looking Beyond Gross Domestic Product (GDP) for a Comprehensive Picture

Looking Beyond Gross Domestic Product (GDP) helps us understand how a country is doing and the kind of development that has been accomplished beyond simply assessing the country's growth. Gross domestic product (GDP) quantifies the monetary worth of all end products and services produced within a nation's borders. However, it needs to provide insight into the allocation of these resources or the makeup of those who benefit from them.

The effects of economic growth on society and the environment are also ignored. Beyond gross domestic product (GDP), various indicators such as income, employment, poverty, educational attainment, and life expectancy can shed light on a country's performance and advancement. Governments and corporations can craft policies that promote long-term success using these metrics. Income data, for instance, can be used to inform poverty alleviation and minimum wage regulations.

Policies to alleviate unemployment or develop vocational education and training programs can be informed by employment data. Investments in education and training programs that give students the skills they'll need for future jobs can be informed by data on educational attainment rates. In addition, life expectancy data can help shape healthcare and equity policy.

Overall, expanding one's focus beyond GDP paints a complete picture of a nation's performance and advancement, which can inform strategic decision-making at the national and corporate levels. Policymakers may develop more effective policies, and firms can make smarter investments that lead to more sustainable growth if they look beyond GDP data to factors like income, employment, poverty, educational attainment, and life expectancy.

Leaders and businesses may better prepare for the future of their respective fields by taking a macro view of the country. Suppose the data shows, for example, that educational attainment rates need to be raised. In that case, policymakers can better understand what has to be done to enhance education to produce a more competent and productive labor force. Similarly, this information can be used by firms to improve the employment security of their staff and their overall competitiveness.

Expanding our view beyond GDP allows us to see the big picture of a country's or company's success and growth. Government officials and businesses can utilize this data to create policies and strategies for long-term growth. Leaders and companies can better serve their residents and employees in the long run when they take a macro picture of the country's predicament. Expanding our focus beyond GDP gives us access to a powerful tool for fostering national and corporate development.

The Role of Philanthropy in Poverty Alleviation

Philanthropy is more than making substantial donations to good causes; it does involve that. Wealthy individuals often establish private foundations to facilitate their philanthropic endeavors. Philanthropy encompasses actions carried out by individuals or groups driven solely by the intention to promote the overall welfare of humanity. Many organizations, including nonprofits that focus on public welfare, medical breakthroughs, education, and human rights, are committed to improving society. Under Section 501(c)(3) of the Internal Revenue Code in the United States, charitable institutions that meet certain requirements are recognized as tax-exempt.

A sustainable society requires a safe economy, secure families, and ample employment opportunities. By funding nonprofits providing vital services to their communities and families, philanthropists may help reduce poverty and expand economic opportunity. Those in most need should receive direct cash transfers, and those who qualify should be linked to benefits that can help them financially. Philanthropists should fund civil society groups to alleviate poverty and promote policies that benefit everyone. Charitable organizations can utilize their visibility and clout to initiate conversations with regional and state governments about investment collaboration. Funding civil society is essential, but foundations should be flexible in their approach so grantees can develop innovative solutions.

Contributions to Society

Giving back to the community has numerous upsides. Experts have found that philanthropy positively affects one's mental and physical health and that donors experience fulfillment from their generosity. Some research suggests that generous people live longer than those who are less generous because they have fewer health problems due to their charitable actions. Giving back to the community has many advantages that go beyond any single person. Companies that give back to the community have numerous benefits, including enhanced brand recognition, public standing, and the possibility of drawing in new business partners and top employees.

In addition, workers who are part of an organization that gives back to the community are more fulfilled and engaged in their roles. Because businesses exist to generate revenue, a notable demonstration of corporate philanthropy can have a positive impact on both existing and potential clientele. Donors in the United States can receive sizable tax breaks in the year they give to charity because of the Charitable Contributions Deduction. On the IRS website, you may get Schedule A, which includes instructions on how to claim this deduction.

Giving and Paying Taxes

Giving to charity does help reduce tax liability, but some people gain more than others. Approximately 60% of AGI is typically tax-deductible per the IRS (AGI). Some extremely affluent people try to avoid paying their fair share of taxes by contributing to charity. However, many claim that billionaires avoid paying their fair share of taxes by using donations to the poor as a cover. As much as $15 billion, or about 5% of all individual contributions, came from the pockets of the nation's wealthiest citizens last year. In the United States, many people donate money to organizations they support. Here are some individuals and organizations actively involved in charitable work. Andrew Carnegie is sometimes cited as the most illustrious philanthropic figure because of the sheer magnitude of his donations. More than 2,500 libraries around the world were funded in part by Carnegie's generosity. Carnegie also established a charitable trust and endowments at various colleges that are still active today, a century after his death in 1919. His overall philanthropic giving is believed to be around $350 million.

Edsel Ford, son of Ford Motor Company founder Henry Ford, established the Ford Foundation to continue his family's tradition of charitable giving. The organization aims to enhance democracy, provide economic opportunities, and better educate the public. The organization's scope includes various fields, such as Participation in Government and Civic Life, Assistive technology, Climate shift, natural resources, and Equal treatment of the sexes, races, and ethnicities.

You can be a philanthropist without being a billionaire or giving away money. There are well-known people whose philanthropic work doesn't require them to be filthy rich. One of the most well-known examples is Mother Teresa. A Catholic nun in Kolkata, India, created the Missionaries of Charity as the Order of the Missionaries of Charity in 1950.

The organization's primary objective was to offer "economic and spiritual welfare" to disadvantaged communities. Billionaire Bill Gates, the co-founder of Microsoft, along with his former spouse Melinda, established the Bill & Melinda Gates Foundation with the intention of financing global assistance and healthcare projects. The group researches and combats disease and poverty worldwide, including in the United States. As stated on its official website, the foundation has given away nearly $54 billion to good causes since 2000.

Philanthropy Ground Cover

Philanthropy and charity are sometimes confused, yet philanthropy encompasses a broader scope. It aims to enhance the long-term welfare of individuals, communities, and whole societies. Many charitable acts are short-term, like providing coats to the homeless in winter, assisting at food pantries, or contributing money to scholarship funds. While these are all generous gestures, they might not meet the criteria for "philanthropic" actions, such as building a library or school or making a substantial contribution to a scholarship program. Warren Buffet, who will turn 93 in January 2024, has donated $46.1 billion. However, you don't need a large fortune to begin supporting worthy causes. Recognizing a philanthropist can result from backing a noble cause with time, effort, and resources. When a business opts to donate funds to a nonprofit or a worthy initiative, it's considered corporate philanthropy. Corporations can contribute in various ways, with monetary donations being the most common. These contributions can take the form of monetary donations, tangible goods, educational opportunities, and active engagement within the community.

There are numerous manifestations of generosity. Both people and businesses can achieve this. Both can occur simultaneously, as is the case when a corporation offers matching donations for all employee contributions. Another option is to leave a bequest in one's will or trust, specifying that a certain amount of money or other assets be donated to a certain charity. Giving to charity can take several forms, including monetary contributions, scholarships, grants, and stipends. Giving to charity is about more than just cash, of course. People may give back by volunteering. Many of the world's billionaires give substantial amounts to nonprofit organizations. It takes work to maintain a high profile. Despite what you might have heard, you don't have to be filthy rich to be a philanthropist. You may think donating a portion of your monthly salary is the only way to make a difference, but this is not the case. One of the best ways to develop philanthropic tendencies is to volunteer for organizations whose missions resonate with you.

Philanthropy Help to Society Blossom

Many of us feel terrible about the plight of the poor in the developing world, but we give up hope because we think we can't do anything to help. The scope of poverty is enormous, yet our ability to address it appears to be limited. While this hopelessness is natural, the statistics tell an entirely different tale. While poverty is severe and pervasive, it is easy to lose sight of how many people live in the developed world and how much impact our donations may have when combined.

An effective charity's ability to aid more people is proportional to the magnitude of their donation. But you don't need to be a millionaire to make a difference; even little contributions can make a big difference in someone's life. A bed net with insecticide to ward off malaria-carrying mosquitoes can be purchased for $2. One cataract surgery to save a person's sight can be purchased for $50. One fistula operation, performed to correct obstetric damage sustained during birth, costs $686.

Philanthropy Helps Those Who Are Most In Need Around The Globe.

Choosing the right charity to donate funds to among the many deserving options can feel overwhelming. But you don't have to navigate this decision alone. The charities listed in The Life You Can Save (provided below) have been carefully chosen through extensive research and analysis by organizations like "GiveWell." These charities are actively involved in addressing a diverse array of crucial issues.

It Makes Money Available For the Poor

The most disadvantaged individuals in the world have a chance to escape poverty with the help of treatments that work. Children can stay healthy and in school if we take steps to prevent and treat disease. When quality healthcare is available to parents, they can continue working to support their families, even in cases of illness or when taking care of their unwell children. Assistance programs play a crucial role in equipping those living in severe destitution with the means to enhance their livelihoods. Giving plays a significant role in the fight against severe poverty, which is an issue with proven remedies. Over the last few decades, there has been a significant reduction in the count of people living in extreme poverty, as evidenced by the evaluation conducted under the framework of the United Nations Millennium Development Goals (MDGs).

Philanthropy Makes Money Available To Fight Poverty.

It's easy to be overwhelmed by the magnitude of human suffering when we learn that many people live in poverty worldwide. However, the aid and relief distribution data paint a totally different picture. We in the wealthy world have access to vast resources, while 767 million people in the developing world struggle to make ends meet on less than $1.90 daily. Considering only the United States, it would only take $3 per citizen to raise $1 billion in humanitarian funds. How much money would be needed annually to provide for the most impoverished people in terms of their basic health and nutrition needs? The rich world has more than enough money to provide for the fundamental necessities of the world's impoverished. The quality of life of potential contributors need not be negatively affected by their generosity, and there is no need to cut funding for healthcare or education in the developed world.

Generosity Boosts Our Mood

According to studies, spending money on oneself does not considerably improve one's pleasure or well-being. According to research conducted at Harvard Business School, those who give to others tend to feel happier themselves. As per the Harvard research findings, a potentially beneficial cycle exists between happiness and generosity. This implies that individuals who are happier tend to exhibit greater generosity, and engaging in acts of giving contributes to an increased sense of happiness.

According to other research, seeing money go to charity makes people happy, even if it isn't your own. However, the greatest joy is felt when people give to charity independently. By giving, we move closer to making the world where we can all thrive. Roughly 10% of humanity consists of the 700 million of us who live on less than $2 a day. No matter how much we'd like to believe that, the reality is that none of us would be where we are now without the availability of food, clean water, shelter, basic healthcare, and political stability—all of which are material circumstances.

Do you want to live in a society where 10% of newborns do not have access to basic health care, clean water, or food because they are among the 700 million people who live on less than $2 per day? There is a clear causal link between inequality and violent crime, which has been repeatedly seen globally and within nations with differing levels of inequality. We can all live in a world that is safer, healthier, more stable, and happier with your help, so please consider donating today.

Seven, Charity Does Good

Many argue that development aid is ineffective since extreme poverty still exists. It has been shown repeatedly that successful aid initiatives cut mortality rates and alleviate suffering in the global South. Independent evaluations are becoming increasingly important for NGOs to boost accountability and fine-tune strategies. Giving What We Can, The Life You Can Save, and GiveWell are just a few groups that provide updated rankings of efficient and effective charities each year.

Charity Depends On Fairness

We all know that no matter how hard we work, elements outside our control always contribute to our success and that our geographic location mostly determines these factors. A person's odds of enjoying a prosperous society's infrastructure, healthcare, education opportunities, and job security rise dramatically if they are born in such a society. Those unfortunate enough to be born in a third-world country have much smaller odds of seeing their efforts pay off. They might not be able to work. They have a medical condition for which they cannot pay. After all, there is no employment available because they lack the knowledge necessary to secure a position that provides a sufficient income, and so on. Just getting through each day is an enormous task.

As a result, citizens in poor countries are frequently at an unfair disadvantage relative to those in more developed nations. Children have no control over their lives, including where they live and whether or not they go to school. Children from low-income families may drop out of school immediately to help bring in money. This helps perpetuate a vicious cycle of poverty that can trap even very bright and diligent individuals held hostage by forces beyond their control. It's a question of basic justice to contribute to causes that alleviate extreme poverty. The world's North-South division starkly illustrates this geographical correlation of social and economic developments. We have a moral imperative to break the cycle of poverty for those born into it once we acknowledge that different circumstances lead to vastly different economic outcomes around the world.

You Can Subtract Your Donation From Your Taxes

In some cases, you may be eligible for a tax deduction if you donate to a nonprofit. Keep an eye out for the receipts the charity sends you at the end of the fiscal year (some do this for every contribution), and file them with your other tax paperwork. To get a tax refund in countries like the United States, you have to itemize your deductions. Because of the tax deduction, your contribution will cost you less. For instance, a taxpayer in the 15 percent tax bracket would save $15 on their taxes if they gave $100 to a qualified charity. If an individual is in the 35 percent tax bracket, their $100 donation will net them $35 after taxes.

Privatization

Privatization is the process through which the government hands over control of an enterprise or an asset to the private sector. The government is no longer the legal owner of the company. What happens when a small group gains control of a publicly traded corporation? Wealth is generated as a result of privatization. Profits rise while production expenses fall. Suppose the government determines that allowing more firms to compete in a certain industry will benefit consumers and the economy. In that case, it is a positive development.

In other words, its primary goal is to improve people's access to services. By taking over particular industries, the government is able to reduce its overall workload. There's no denying the global impact privatization has had. Living here has advantages and disadvantages, just like there are two sides to a coin. The primary argument favoring privatization is that for-profit businesses are incentivized to maximize efficiency and minimize spending. Managers in government-controlled industries typically do not receive a cut of the company's earnings. However, a private company has profit in mind, so it is more likely to prioritize efficiency and cost-cutting. Companies like B.T. and British Airways have become more efficient and profitable since becoming privatized.

There are various ways in which a country's economy can benefit from the privatization of state-owned firms. Efficiency gains, more competition, easier access to finance and technology, enhanced corporate governance, and a rise in overseas investment are just a few of the many upsides. Privatization leads to greater productivity because private enterprises are not constrained by the same rules as public ones. They can streamline their processes and boost their revenue as a result. Because of this, more jobs can be made available, and workers' pay can rise, which is good for the economy as a whole.

As privatized businesses vie for customers and market share, competition rises as a byproduct. More options are good for business because they spur innovation and ultimately benefit consumers. The general growth of a country's economy benefits from privatization because private businesses have greater access to funding and advanced technologies. Companies can grow their operations and create more jobs when they have more money to invest in growing their firm.

Privatization promotes stronger corporate governance since private owners are typically more accountable for their decisions than governmental ones. This aids in maintaining shareholder rights and promoting market openness. When a country is privatized, it becomes more appealing to potential foreign investors, who may then decide to invest there. Increased economic growth and employment opportunities are possible outcomes of this infusion of funds. There are several ways in which privatization might help a country's economy. Privatizing state-owned firms can positively affect a country's economy and people, including more efficiency and competition, easier resource access, and more foreign investment.

Governments need to be more effective at handling the economy. Political factors, rather than considerations of efficiency and profitability, drive their actions. A wasteful use of resources would be employing extra people in a state-owned company. The government may hesitate to fire the employees because of the bad press associated with layoffs. Therefore, too many people are employed by state-owned firms, leading to wasteful practices. The next election is always on a government's mind. Since short-term electoral gains are paramount, business leaders may be reluctant to invest in infrastructure upgrades that might benefit the company in the long run. Different from frontline services like healthcare, public sector investment may be easily reduced. Wealth is generated as a result of privatization. Profits rise while production expenses fall. If the government determines that allowing more firms to compete in a certain industry will benefit consumers and the economy, then it is a positive development.

Engaging Nonprofits, Foundations, and Corporations in Poverty Solutions

Multiple avenues exist through which businesses, foundations, and nonprofit organizations can join forces to combat poverty. These entities possess the resources to provide individuals in deprived circumstances with opportunities for accessing necessities such as food, healthcare, education, and job prospects, which might otherwise remain inaccessible due to their impoverished conditions. To better understand poverty and its causes and to develop solutions to overcome them, research studies might be funded by philanthropic organizations, foundations, and businesses.

Organizations like charities, philanthropies, and businesses can also lend a hand by providing free labor or personnel to get projects done. Public outreach initiatives can increase the number of individuals who learn about the issue of poverty and who take action to alleviate it. The struggle against poverty is one in which nonprofits, foundations, and companies can make a substantial impact. Although governments and people play critical roles, these groups have access to significantly greater resources. Long-term, sustainable change can be achieved through strategic alliances, well-directed investments, and novel approaches.

Providing financial backing to programs that aim to better the lives of individuals living in extreme poverty, philanthropic organizations like foundations and nonprofits play a vital role in helping to relieve poverty. The health, education, economic opportunity, and other services lacking in low-wealth communities are generally the focus of foundation contributions. Donations from individuals and businesses help nonprofits support programs that address particular social problems, such as helping entrepreneurs in disadvantaged communities get their enterprises off the ground or giving access to quality education for children from low-income families.

Businesses may play a significant role in reducing poverty through their operations. Initiatives for corporate social responsibility allow businesses to help others and improve society. Many businesses give money and time to charity to fight poverty, and some participate in initiatives that aim to improve low-income communities' economic situation. In addition, some businesses may collaborate with governments and nonprofits to construct permanent programs that give people in severe poverty sustainable development opportunities.

Combating poverty is an uphill struggle that needs constant attention. Long-term solutions require the combined efforts of governments, citizens, and corporations. NGOs, endowments, and businesses can contribute significantly by funding creative approaches to addressing poverty. By working together and making wise investments, they can strengthen local communities and provide access to economic possibilities that will have a long-lasting impact. There is a significant role for corporations, foundations, and nonprofits in fighting poverty. By investing in innovative strategies that target the root causes of poverty and establishing strategic partnerships with governments and various organizations, they have the potential to create tangible and impactful changes in the lives of individuals. They may make long-lasting progress toward a more egalitarian society by financing initiatives that provide access to jobs, healthcare, and learning opportunities. These groups can make a huge impact in the fight against poverty, provided they are fully dedicated and given adequate resources.

CHAPTER SEVEN

THE INTERCONNECTEDNESS OF WEALTH CREATION STRATEGIES

Understanding the synergy between diverse wealth generation methods is of paramount importance. Consider, for instance, the integration of stocks and bonds into a diversified portfolio that can culminate in financial stability. An equally vital approach involves setting aside funds for unforeseen expenses or channeling resources toward debt reduction, both of which contribute to augmenting your financial gains.

Undoubtedly, the prowess of compound interest should be considered. This financial phenomenon ensures that your initial investment burgeons as accrued interest is reinvested, magnifying your eventual yield. Such a mechanism paves the way for achieving long-term objectives without necessitating immediate sacrifices from wealth-generation workers.

Strategic use of tax mechanisms, including 401(k) plans and Roth IRAs, can significantly bolster wealth accumulation. By adeptly managing tax strategies, it becomes feasible to judiciously oversee your financial resources and retain a greater portion of your earnings. Employing these fiscal avenues enables wealth creators to optimize their profits while concurrently mitigating potential risks, all within a meticulously structured financial blueprint.

Strategies for creating wealth are interrelated in different ways. While each tactic should be considered independently, knowing how they interact can lead to better long-term decisions and performance. If one takes the time to craft a comprehensive financial strategy, one can increase their chances of success in building wealth in all areas. Wealth makers can maximize their efficiency and effectiveness in creating and amassing wealth by adopting a holistic approach. If they can see how different tactics work together, they will have access to higher return potentials, which will ultimately help them achieve their goals. After all, it takes more than one plan to secure a prosperous future financially; you need an all-encompassing strategy.

The government serves as the initial catalyst for the journey towards economic prosperity. In an economy characterized by favorable economic policies, legal frameworks, and investment choices, businesses are inclined to foster innovation and provide products and services that align with consumer needs and preferences. When these companies succeed, they attract investors who help finance their expansion, which creates more jobs and higher wages, which are good for the economy. Profits rise as more of a company's offerings are purchased by consumers. They are able to adapt to the ever-changing market because of their continued investment in R&D. However, the first step in creating wealth is for each person to take charge of his or her financial circumstances.

Everyone has the ability to begin building money for themselves through budgeting, saving, investing, or entrepreneurship. It is possible to save substantial money for retirement or other long-term goals if one plans with diligence and forethought. The engine that propels our economy is this web of interdependence between the various means of creating wealth. There is a positive ripple effect that helps everyone when people take charge of their financial future. A thriving society that prioritizes the pursuit of financial freedom via hard labor and sensible investments requires the joint efforts of governments, corporations, and individuals. With these methods, everyone can start on the path to wealth building and have a more comfortable financial future.

The chain of events leading to wealth creation begins with governments enacting sensible economic laws, continues with businesses seizing profitable investment opportunities, and finishes with each person taking charge of his or her financial situation. We can more efficiently lay the groundwork for a more robust economy that benefits all of us if we know how each part impacts the others. With these methods in mind, we may build money that will last many years.

Investigating the Relationship Between Individual and National Prosperity

The distribution of wealth and income pertains to how a country's resources are allocated among its citizens or how global resources are divided among sovereign states. Analyzing and understanding these distribution patterns involves employing statistical methods that rely on varying reliability data. A person's wealth is calculated by combining their assets and the value of their claims on those assets. Assigning a monetary value requires determining prices for each item, which can pose challenges when items are not easily marketable due to their condition.

Earnings encompass the total income received within a specified timeframe. In some nations, wealth statistics are sourced from mandatory assessments of the estates of recently deceased individuals, which may not accurately reflect the possessions of the living. In many countries, annual tax returns serve as a proxy for income and are thus considered a credible data source.

However, making comparisons is complicated by differing definitions of income, including whether to include non-productive activity-related transfers, capital gains, or losses that impact an individual's wealth.

A standardized approach is essential for categorizing national income and wealth distributions. One effective classification method involves attributing wealth and income to factors of production such as wages, rent, interest, and profit, corresponding to labor, land, and capital ownership, respectively. These wealth and income statistics are generally presented per capita and are often derived from tax reports.

The average annual income of a population can be roughly estimated using the concept of gross national income (GNI) per capita. The gross national product (GNI) per person in highly developed nations is significantly higher than in less developed nations. For instance, in the twenty-first century's first decade, the World Bank calculated that the per-capita gross national income (GNI) was more than $10,000 in the most developed countries and less than $825 in the least developed countries. There is also a wide range in national income.

Even in a wealthy nation like the United States, there is a wide gap in wealth distribution between different occupations, regions, rural and urban areas, sexes, and ethnic groups. While most Americans live comfortably on an income from work, median pay varies widely by industry. (Compare GDP, GDP, and gross national product.) Higher incomes in an economy will be driven more by investment than by wage increases. The proportion of revenue from investments tends to grow in proportion to overall income.

Because most fortunes take decades to amass, a class of extremely affluent people can emerge if they are able to hold on to their wealth and pass it on to future generations. A distinct type of inheritance affects earned incomes. Education and opportunity are primary drivers of economic mobility and social mobility. As a result, it is not uncommon for the offspring of wealthy families who also happen to be highly educated to continue in their parent's footsteps. However, in a dynamic economy, success is more likely to be achieved through one's efforts.

Reversing Inflation

Inflation arises when the expenditure on goods and services surpasses the overall output. Price hikes might result from limitations in supply that escalate the expenses of manufacturing goods and providing services or due to consumers spending more money than producers can generate, often linked to a growing economy. The combination of these two circumstances typically causes inflation. Governments usually strive to keep inflation at a reasonable range that promotes growth without drastically reducing the currency's value. The primary obligation for curbing inflation within the United States lies with the Federal Open Market Committee (FOMC), a sector of the Federal Reserve responsible for formulating monetary policies aimed at realizing the Fed's objectives of maintaining price stability and achieving optimal employment levels.

For a variety of reasons, keeping inflation in check may be difficult. When prices are higher, workers want higher salaries. It is theoretically possible for workers to receive better pay because they can purchase more goods, leading to a wage-price spiral. As a result, demand grows, and prices rise. Inflation is particularly challenging to control since measures to prevent it, but if the following strategies are implemented, it will reflect on the economy.

a. Compulsory Business Reserves

The reserve mandate signifies the minimum quantity of physical currency that financial institutions must retain, whether within their own secure vaults or the adjacent Federal Reserve Bank. This measure is intended to ensure sufficient funds are available to meet customer deposits. For businesses, adhering to reserve requirements is a regulatory mandate and a strategic tool in the Federal Reserve's arsenal to regulate inflationary pressures within the economy.

In times of economic expansion, the Federal Reserve can opt for an expansionary monetary policy by lowering the reserve requirement. Conversely, during periods of economic contraction, an increase in the reserve requirement serves as a contractionary measure. This latter approach effectively reduces liquidity in the market, consequently moderating economic activity.

The determination of the reserve requirement rests with the board of governors at the Federal Reserve. This requirement stands as one of the cornerstones of monetary policy, alongside open market operations and the discount rate. Various financial institutions, including banks, credit unions, savings and loan associations, Edge Act corporations, agreement corporations, and the American branches and agencies of international banks, all fall under the ambit of these reserve regulations.

b. Mandatory/Increased Savings For High-Income Earners

Making saving a requirement is now an effective approach to lower inflation. A contractionary policy aims to lower the amount of money in an economy by increasing interest rates. As a result, credit becomes more expensive, which reduces consumer and business spending and slows economic growth. Higher interest rates on government securities also impede growth by incentivizing banks and investors to buy Treasuries, which offer a fixed rate of return, rather than riskier equity investments, which profit from low interest rates.

c. Enhanced Goods and Services Production

Supply-side strategies are oriented towards fostering sustained productivity growth and bolstering overall competitiveness. Initiatives such as deregulation and privatization have been advanced with the aim of enhancing corporate efficiency and market competitiveness. By harnessing these supply-side tools, it is envisaged that the economy's capacity to generate goods and services will be heightened, contributing to long-term economic vitality.

The anticipated consequence of supply-side interventions is the mitigation of long-term inflationary pressures. While these measures are not inherently designed to curtail immediate inflation spikes, they can potentially diminish inflation over time. It's essential to note that the efficacy of government-led supply-side endeavors in quelling inflation is not assured. Success hinges on various factors and is contingent upon the intricate interplay of economic dynamics.

The essence of supply-side regulations lies in their capacity to augment competitiveness over extended horizons. An illustrative example is the implementation of privatization and deregulation, both of which hold the potential to streamline business operations and mitigate operational costs. By fortifying businesses in this manner, these measures ultimately contribute to alleviating inflationary pressures in the long run.

d. Increased Loan Requirements

During the early 1980s, the United Kingdom adopted a form of monetarism characterized by the government's endeavor to curtail inflation by constricting money circulation. This approach involved the implementation of elevated interest rates and a reduction in the budget deficit, both aimed at regulating the overall money supply within the economy. While this course of action did lead to a reduction in inflation, it came at a considerable cost, plunging the nation into a profound recession.

Fostering Local Investments and Local Content/Consumption

The measure by which economic growth is assessed is the gross domestic product (GDP), which signifies the combined annual worth of all goods and services produced within a country. The dynamics shaping economic growth are multifaceted and intricate. It's important to recognize that while no singular factor can ensure the ideal or optimal pace of growth for an economy, certain strategies hold the potential to drive it forward. Among these strategies, one stands out: bolstering support for local businesses.

Local business support serves as a catalyst for a series of positive economic outcomes. It triggers the expansion of industries, thereby contributing to the economy's overall growth. This, in turn, translates into job creation, addressing a critical need for employment opportunities, particularly for those currently unemployed. Such endeavors align with the broader objectives of productivity enhancement and holistic economic advancement.

Elevating employment rates stands as a pivotal route towards poverty alleviation. Introducing more job opportunities within local communities lays the foundation for eradicating poverty. This approach provides individuals with financial stability and fosters a sense of empowerment and inclusivity within society.

Recognizing the intricate interplay of these elements underscores the significance of a comprehensive approach to economic development. While GDP offers a quantifiable measure of growth, it's imperative to remember that true progress extends beyond mere numbers. It involves the creation of meaningful opportunities, the strengthening of local enterprises, and the upliftment of entire communities. By investing in local businesses, cultivating local consumption patterns, and strategically generating employment opportunities, nations can embark on a path of sustainable growth that encompasses the well-being of all citizens.

Recognizing Synergies Across Sectors

There should be global cooperation between governments, corporations, and nonprofits to combat poverty. Synergies can be discovered by identifying strategic areas where cross-sector collaboration and innovation can benefit low-income communities. Partnerships involving enterprises from varying nations, for instance, have the potential to combine resources and diverse viewpoints to tackle challenges associated with poverty. Moreover, governments, corporations, and social initiatives can identify possible synergies concerning improved access to healthcare, education, and employment opportunities. These organizations are better able to make a difference in the world when they join forces in partnerships that benefit both parties.

In addition, it is easier to find and execute solutions suited to individual communities' requirements when governments, corporations, and other organizations work together. Furthermore, such partnerships can assemble a wide range of interested parties and give rise to new growth and economic development possibilities in underprivileged regions. Governments, businesses, and other groups can work together to solve the global poverty problem long-term by recognizing synergies across sectors.

All organizations should recognize the benefit of collaboration in fighting global poverty. By pooling resources and thinking creatively about combatting issues like poverty, synergistic collaborations between government, business, and social organizations may make a real difference for people everywhere. Positive results can be achieved via collaboration and innovation when these organizations bring their varied perspectives to bear on the problem of global poverty. We can find long-term answers to the problem of global poverty if we can see the connections between different fields of work.

The needs of the poor can only be satisfied via concerted efforts by the government, the business community, and social service organizations. If these groups work together, progress can be made toward universal access to economic growth and development resources, including education, healthcare, and employment opportunities. Governments, corporations, and nonprofits can all do their part to fight global poverty by learning from one another and working together. Deeply ingrained issues affecting communities experiencing poverty can be addressed and remedied by recognizing synergies across sectors and building meaningful working partnerships with each other.

To effectively combat global poverty, all relevant parties must acknowledge the importance of collaboration. By pooling resources and thinking creatively about combatting issues like poverty, synergistic collaborations between government, business, and social organizations may make a real difference for people everywhere. We can develop effective strategies to alleviate global poverty by identifying cross-sectoral synergies. If these groups work together, progress can be made toward universal access to economic growth and development resources, including education, healthcare, and employment opportunities.

Together, we have a much better chance of bringing down worldwide poverty rates. It is essential to identify cross-sector synergies to reduce global poverty. If we want real change in our world, collaborating between governments, corporations, and other groups will take collaboration. We have the chance to establish long-lasting solutions that can reduce global poverty if we know how to leverage resources best and innovate around the difficulties associated with poverty. To reduce global poverty, it will be necessary for all actors to realize the need for collaboration. Global economic growth and development require universal access to quality education, healthcare, and employment opportunities; with their combined efforts, we can get a long way toward this goal. We can only help those in need worldwide if we pool our resources and efforts.

Exploring How Nations Can Cooperate and Collaborate

Thriving in today's globally interlinked landscape necessitates proactively pursuing collaborative opportunities among nations. A comprehensive grasp of the global economy coupled with adeptness at international cooperation serve as foundational requisites for the effective formulation of economic strategies on a state-to-state basis.

The mechanism of trade agreements exemplifies the essence of international cooperation. Such accords typically entail the elimination of tariffs, non-tariff restrictions, quotas, and subsidies, thereby fostering a seamless exchange of goods between the signatories nations. The outcome is access to untapped markets and an enhanced production capacity at reduced costs, courtesy of diminished trade barriers—a mutual gain for all participating countries.

In the pursuit of cooperative economic progress, countries can adopt approaches that involve joint investment and the establishment of trade alliances. One such avenue is the channel of direct foreign investment, wherein a business entity from one nation acquires assets within another. A parallel avenue is manifested through joint ventures, where companies from distinct countries collaborate to establish an entirely new entity. Both pathways facilitate the amalgamation of national resources and financial capital, thus enabling the foray into new consumer markets.

These collaborative endeavors, whether through trade agreements, foreign investments, or joint ventures, underscore the potency of collective action in economic advancement. By transcending national boundaries, pooling resources, and aligning interests, nations can collectively leverage opportunities to harness growth, innovation, and prosperity for their citizens.

At long last, nations may work together for the common good by forging strategic alliances. Two or more countries work together on infrastructure and innovation as part of these collaborations. Industry development in developing countries can benefit from such partnerships, while chances for technological or economic advancement in more developed countries can be created. Global collaboration is crucial for the economic development of any nation. Countries can access additional resources and expand into more lucrative markets by collaborating on trade deals, investments, and strategic alliances.

Cooperation between countries can help reduce poverty and its consequences. International cooperation and coordination is one approach. International actors can pool their resources and devise plans to combat global poverty. These actors include governments, NGOs, multilateral organizations, private enterprises, philanthropists, and individuals. Improving infrastructure in underdeveloped countries is one area where nations could work together to alleviate poverty. This may involve constructing new roads, installing water and sewage systems, enhancing existing schools or hospitals, or providing other medical care. Developing countries may eventually become self-sufficient if developed nations provide technological aid in agricultural production and financial administration.

Trade is another area in which we work together. By accepting their goods, governments can increase their economic potential and help developing nations. Developing nations would benefit from tariff elimination or the implementation of preferential trading arrangements in the global market.

Children, women, refugees, and the oppressed could all benefit from international cooperation to enact protective measures. Laws protecting employees from exploitation, better healthcare, and social services fall under this category. International cooperation on environmentally friendly initiatives is possible.

The development of economies could benefit from measures such as creating renewable energy and conserving natural resources. All of these situations demonstrate how international collaboration and cooperation can be an efficient method for fighting poverty. By combining efforts and resources, countries can accomplish more than they could on their own. In this way, those currently mired in poverty can have a shot at bettering their circumstances and providing for their families.

Reviving poverty reduction gains will require policies that boost economic growth across the board, not only in the world's poorest nations but also in those in the middle-income range. In these unpredictable times, measures encouraging private sector activity across the economy will be essential for generating investment, creating jobs, and reducing poverty. To begin making the necessary course corrections, policies can be helpful if they are well conceived and carried out. Policymakers must do everything possible to end extreme poverty and prevent further setbacks.

Implementation Challenges and Opportunities

Addressing global poverty is an imperative task that demands immediate attention. The reverberations of poverty extend across individuals, communities, and even entire nations, rendering it a multifaceted challenge. While commendable strides have been made in mitigating poverty, substantial operational hurdles persist. The need for more available resources poses a formidable barrier to effective poverty alleviation initiatives. Limited financial reservoirs within most countries impede the efficacy of anti-poverty programs. With adequate financial backing, the ability to uplift living conditions and enact poverty-reducing strategies is greatly improved.

Accessing additional funds from international donors or organizations is marred by bureaucratic entanglements and stringent recipient criteria, rendering the process exceedingly arduous. Implementing poverty reduction measures is further complicated by the innate human resistance to change. Individuals, particularly those in rural areas, often exhibit apprehension toward abandoning established routines. Cultural influences can also contribute to reluctance in endorsing projects that necessitate shifts in habits or routines. Prior to the successful implementation of any initiatives, comprehensive community engagement is crucial, ensuring awareness of plans and potential challenges.

The technological landscape introduces a plethora of challenges in executing poverty reduction programs. Limited technology access, inadequate infrastructure, a need for more skilled personnel, and difficulties in reaching remote areas are prominent obstacles that impede effective implementation. Yet, amid these challenges, numerous opportunities await countries to combat poverty through effective programs. A noteworthy example is the establishment of social safety nets, ensuring access to healthcare, education, and a basic income. Additional avenues include investment in infrastructure, enhancing credit accessibility or introducing microfinance initiatives, and creating localized employment opportunities.

For governments, NGOs, the business sector, and development partners to achieve their respective goals, meticulous planning and seamless coordination are imperative. Such a comprehensive strategy must encompass every facet of poverty alleviation endeavors, from initial planning to comprehensive evaluation. Addressing poverty is a complex endeavor, necessitating an approach that holistically accounts for all the interconnected components. By doing so, nations can foster equitable and prosperous societies, dismantling barriers to success.

Eliminating poverty emerges as a pressing global concern, and its successful implementation encounters multifarious hurdles. From financial constraints to resistance against change and technological hindrances, the road to poverty alleviation is rife with challenges. However, various constructive approaches exist, including social safety nets, skills training programs, enhanced credit access, microfinance initiatives, and infrastructure investments. Ultimately, a comprehensive strategy that considers each dynamic of poverty reduction—from initial planning to outcome assessment—is pivotal.

The realization of more just and prosperous societies hinges upon meticulous planning and cohesive collaboration among diverse stakeholders. Through orchestrated efforts, countries can usher in a future where equal opportunities are extended to all, propelling humanity closer to a world free from poverty.

Identifying Political, Economic, and Social Barriers to Success

Poverty is a multifaceted problem from numerous societal, political, and cultural influences. Consequently, more than relying solely on economic strategies is needed to alleviate poverty; a comprehensive and synchronized approach is necessary. This is, in fact, the thinking behind many different approaches to alleviating poverty. Then what are the concerns? Because strong and sustainable rates of economic growth require macroeconomic stability, and economic growth is the single most important factor impacting poverty. Therefore, a policy to reduce poverty should prioritize maintaining macroeconomic stability. The global problem of poverty has persisted for a long time, and its elimination will not come easily. This essay will examine the political, economic, and social obstacles that prevent global poverty from being eliminated.

The classic definition of political instability is a government's propensity to fall apart due to internal strife or excessive rivalry among political parties. A government transition also enhances the chance of further shifts in leadership. Instability in political leadership is often endemic. Political stability and economic expansion go hand in hand. However, investment and economic growth could slow due to the unpredictability caused by a volatile political climate.

On the contrary, when the economy functions suboptimally, governmental instability and political turbulence are possible. Yet, to ensure political stability, authorities may resort to methods such as repression or orchestrating the victory of a particular political party in subsequent elections. However, political stability dynamics are multifaceted and can have varying implications. While political stability is a coveted state, it can inadvertently foster cronyism due to the lack of accountability for unethical conduct. This phenomenon underscores the complexity faced by numerous nations grappling with fragile political systems.

Political calm has been the exception rather than the rule throughout human history. All political systems, even democracies, are precarious. If a country is free from war and sudden leadership changes do not threaten its citizens, then its citizens can put their minds to more productive uses. The current empirical literature has uncovered many variables that substantially correlate with corruption. Long-standing democracies and stable governments are protective against corruption. However, many countries in the modern world feature a combination of the two strongest drivers of corruption: established autocracies and fledgling democracies.

Some people believe that political stability discourages citizens and prevents any positive change from happening. Creativity and originality are put on the back burner. Many people want things to alter in the spheres of politics, commerce, and culture so that they might live better and have more possibilities in the future. Modifying something is always a gamble. However, it must be done. Complacency and stagnation that prevent competition are also symptoms of political stability. The rules of competition are applicable in many contexts beyond the commercial world.

Competition can be applied to any field, including government, academia, industry, creativity, and the arts. When we talk about a country being politically stable, we're referring to the little serious opposition to the ruling elite. The 'politically stable' regime strictly enforces limits on individual liberty. Press freedom, religious liberty, internet use, and the ability to express political criticism are all curtailed similarly. This can lead to corruption and power abuse.

Political Barriers

The elimination of poverty can be hampered by factors such as political instability and corruption. Disruption to the economy and a subsequent rise in poverty can result from war, terrorism, and other forms of violent conflict. Corruption is another barrier to economic growth, and the government's lack of openness and accountability only exacerbates the problem. Poorer citizens' voices may not be heard or their rights honored if they do not have access to democratic mechanisms. Governments in developing nations may need more tools and access to funding to address poverty effectively. The transmission of funding into poverty-reduction projects is hampered in many of these countries due to a lack of the requisite infrastructure. Some administrations may also need more robust institutions committed to efficient governance and infrastructure management, which can further slow development. Further, corruption and political upheaval in some nations can thwart attempts at genuine reform.

Economic Barriers

There are also significant monetary hurdles to reducing poverty. Lack of capital and investment opportunities can be a serious problem, as it hinders enterprises' growth and creates jobs for those who would otherwise be unable to afford them. Large trade deficits are a common problem for poor countries, hindering their capacity to sell competitively priced commodities and slowing economic progress. When working to alleviate poverty around the world, stagnant earnings and weak purchasing power pose additional challenges.

The disparity between the wealth of some nations and others has long been a factor in the world's overall poverty rate. Poorer countries cannot receive aid and develop their economies because of the imbalance of power caused by inequality. Economic policies undertaken by more developed countries often disadvantage poorer countries in trade practices and access to global markets, exacerbating the problem. International financial institution-implemented structural adjustment programs may hinder efforts to eradicate poverty by prioritizing spending cuts over initiatives to boost the economy and create or redistribute jobs.

Social Barrier

Efforts towards poverty eradication face a series of intricate social challenges that necessitate careful attention and resolution. A notable impediment is the need for more access to education, prevalent in certain nations, which can curtail individuals from accessing quality employment opportunities and hinder the expansion of their economies. Moreover, gender-based discrimination perpetuates a cycle that restricts the advancement of women and girls, thereby perpetuating gender inequality. This hindrance not only obstructs their potential but also undermines broader societal progress.

The repercussions of such barriers ripple across various domains. Limited access to economic and political systems impedes meaningful participation, amplifying existing disparities. Ethnic differences and minority status further compound these inequities, exacerbating poverty in diverse regions across the globe.

Poverty, affecting millions, requires a united response that transcends borders. Collaboration between national governments and international organizations is paramount in tackling these multifaceted challenges. By addressing political, economic, and social hurdles, we can pave the way toward a future where poverty is no longer insurmountable. In this discourse, we've examined key obstacles that demand resolution to usher in a world free from the shackles of poverty.

Overcoming Cultural Resistance to Change

You should know that money, how we use it, and how we talk about it can be seen quite differently across cultures before you open your wallet, get into that negotiation, or even just strike up a casual discussion abroad. To help you avoid losing a transaction, a friendship, or that vase in the window because of cultural differences in how we talk about and handle money, I've included some instances from my experiences working in over 100 countries.

During a price negotiation, Swedish businessman Lars became frustrated when his Saudi business partner Ahmed began with an opening price that was too high, and he expected to be bullied by Lars into proposing a lesser price. Lars felt insulted and thought he had wasted his time throughout the process, while Ahmed thought Lars wasn't serious about the discussion. The negotiation was doomed before it began because of divergent cultural expectations of what a negotiation entails. While Swedes and other Scandinavians place a premium on making "reasonable" offers that benefit all parties, Saudis and other Gulf Arabs anticipate bargaining, applying a "win-lose" attitude with strangers and a "win-win" attitude only with close friends and allies.

The long-term relationship is more important than the immediate terms on the table in Gulf Arabian business negotiations; if this is a one-time opportunity, both parties will be looking to come out on top. Establish your demands up front, listen and probe for their hidden wants, offer reasonable answers, and expect them to offer acceptable solutions if you're doing business in Sweden. Avoid haggling since it gives the impression that you are trying to get a better deal than what you offer. That shows a lack of trust since it means you would have rather the other party pay more than they should have if you had gotten your first price. This is not acceptable behavior in Stockholm for conducting business.

Wu was excited to meet John, his new buddy from the United States, and John was happy to make a new friend during his first trip to China over tea in a fancy Shanghai tea shop. Wu's English was adequate for a casual discussion, and John was excited to meet him despite the language barrier. John was taken aback when Wu, curious to learn more about him, said, "So John, how much money do you make in your job?" John disliked giving a detailed response since he found the question intrusive. Wu was offended that John wasn't being forthright with his response.

To make matters worse, Wu tensed and grew uncomfortable when John asked him the same question to develop a relationship based on equality between them. This meeting, which had started with the greatest intentions, was quickly disintegrating into an adversarial relationship, and neither participant understood what to do about it. But if John had known about Chinese culture (and Wu about Western society), he would have recognized that talking about money is a manner of opening up to the other person and not something private to keep from them. Money is a constant topic of conversation in China, whether it is how much someone makes, how much they cost, the price of goods, how to save money, or how to make money.

In China, relationships are typically established based on our roles and situations' comparability — or equality —. In contrast, in the West, relationships are established based on the disparity of the duties we have with each other and the commitments that lead from those role differences. Because you have the financial resources to do so and because you have committed to the other person by entering into a relationship, you may feel obligated to do so if you are the higher earner in the pair. Because Wu was probably making less money than John (the foreign tourist in China), Wu was probably curious about John's salary. Still, it would have been embarrassing for Wu to reveal his lower salary information to John. John's inquiry into Wu's financial situation was inappropriate. Still, in his view, he was simply being fair: if sensitive concerns regarding Wu's earnings were to be "on the table," then John would have to do the same. However, in China, Wu simply "lost face," an extremely humiliating and difficult-to-recover-from situation that can severely destroy an emerging relationship.

Just what was John supposed to do? Though it was culturally expected in China, he may have felt more at ease explaining the bigger picture without discussing his salary. He might have said, "Well, in my country, people who do my kind of work typically earn between XXX and YYY dollars per year, but you know, in the U.S., college tuition can cost about XXX, and houses can cost about XXX, and healthcare costs about xxx, and so, at the end of the year, I don't have any money left!" Information was shared, friendship was maintained, and there were no assumed commitments.

Lucy, while they were having drinks at a café near the Grande Place in Brussels, said that "CEO wages over here in Belgium is considered more as compensation for the work they perform, like any other employee in the firm, and not a reward based on company shareholder value." She elaborated, "In reality, it would be seen as indecent, even repulsive, to pay a CEO a hundred times what the ordinary person makes here in Belgium."

Some Americans, I've been told, view efforts to ensure that all workers, and by extension, all citizens, have access to healthcare, maternal and paternal rights, free education, etc., as some sort of biblical evil that goes against natural law, as if markets were a natural ph. "In our country, not providing these basic human services by a company would be seen as an abdication of the company's or the government's responsibilities to provide for its employees or its people; in your country, it would be seen as government overreach and the creation of a "nanny-state" for people who won't do for themselves. I don't understand why people in your country have such a view; it's common knowledge that not everyone has the same access to resources and that governments and businesses have responsibilities to protect fundamental human rights. Even if it has a high price. People pay a lot in taxes but get the services they need and expect.

How people on either side of the Atlantic Ocean see money, taxes, and the function of government are fundamentally different. In Europe, at least since the Enlightenment, citizens have generally looked to their government to provide for their basic needs and safeguard their rights; in the United States, which had a revolution in 1776 against all things European, the government is often viewed as a burden that should be avoided if at all possible.

Of course, these are just two extremes on a spectrum, and some groups advocate differently on both sides of the Atlantic (e.g., Democrats and Republicans in the United States, and socialists and democrats in Europe), but the historical and cultural differences between the two regions explain why the center of gravity is different. Therefore, money and work are seen as a means to an end (work to live) in the traditional European perspective, whereas in the United States, they are commonly seen as ends in and of themselves (live to work).

It's crucial to remember that in many societies, working is not about making money but creating a safe, welcoming community where everyone, not just myself, can thrive. Salary and wealth may not be the primary motivator for work, at least for employees and staff in these cultures (Scandinavia, Japan, Netherlands, Malaysia, Thailand, Switzerland, Singapore, much of Latin America, and others); rather, the degree to which I can have a comfortable work environment and relationship with my associates daily may be more important. In Thailand, for instance, there is a term called "senuke" that may be loosely translated as "fun"; work, like everything else in life, ought to be senuke, or at least enjoyable, and any manager in Thailand should make creating a working atmosphere that is senuke for staff a top priority.

Maintaining positive relationships with coworkers is sometimes more important than bringing in a few additional baht monthly. In these societies, the short-term benefits of working in a stressful environment often outweigh the long-term costs to employers and employees. Dealing with the inherent cultural differences in how we deal with money, wealth, and even the very nature of work is necessary in today's global world, and this is true whether you're negotiating or not. These cultural differences are true; we cannot eliminate them, and we need to handle and respect them, even if we don't like them, don't understand them, or disapprove of them.

Embracing a Culture of Inclusion and Collaboration

Business, government, and cooperation organizations are prime positioned to effect positive global change. They can reduce poverty by adopting a spirit of mutual aid and cooperation. These organizations may make significant progress in reducing inequality and enhancing global well-being by, among other things, giving financial assistance and establishing economic opportunities for neglected communities. As a means of combating poverty, inclusivity is essential.

To effectively combat poverty, businesses and governments must thoroughly understand the economic, social, and cultural variables that play a role. Including more people in the decision-making process increases the likelihood of finding answers specific to regional problems. Enhancing access to opportunities for marginalized communities involves businesses adopting equitable recruitment practices and actively promoting a workforce that embraces diversity.

Governments and corporations, on the other hand, can be compelling voices for reform. They can lobby for policy measures that increase economic participation by forming coalitions with other interested parties. Governments should support social initiatives that positively affect poverty reduction and promote public-private partnerships to harness private resources. Corporations and cooperative groups also ensure their activities do not exacerbate poverty or exploitative conditions. This entails conducting background checks, assuring compliance with labor regulations, and providing adequate compensation and working conditions for all staff members.

Investment in community projects and the development of new economic prospects are two ways in which businesses can help to strengthen underserved areas. Cooperation between companies and governments is crucial for achieving successful poverty reduction. When they work together, stakeholders can pool their resources and expertise to find innovative solutions. Communities living in poverty should be actively involved in this effort since their perspectives can shed light on local issues and provide ways to address them.

Several things must be worked on to establish a cooperative and welcoming atmosphere. The first step toward making our society welcoming is to value differences. Opportunities for creative, ground-breaking ideas can arise when people from disparate backgrounds work together on a single project or campaign. Furthermore, including these varying points of view in the formulation of laws and practices can help produce a more equal society.

All people should be afforded the same chances at fulfillment. Education, job-readiness courses, and other public services fall under this category. Initiating programs that encourage a welcoming and diverse work environment is also essential. This includes setting policies that support a varied representation in decision-making processes, giving training on cultural competency, and building mentorship programs for marginalized individuals. Collaboration between different industries should be encouraged in addition to diversity and inclusion efforts. There is a gulf between non-governmental organizations (NGOs), governments, and corporations in developing programs to help people experiencing poverty. Together, these organizations may pool their strengths and develop innovative approaches to resolving the core causes of poverty in local communities worldwide.

Last, we must work for a world where everyone has safe, affordable, and equitable access to food, shelter, and medical care. The government and nonprofits can collaborate to help needy people receive these benefits. Furthermore, businesses have the potential to collaborate with nonprofit organizations and similar entities to guarantee the widespread availability of education, training, and resources necessary for individuals to thrive in the contemporary economy. The only way to effectively combat global poverty is to foster a culture of openness and cooperation.

Together, we can break down barriers and develop programs that provide people in low-income areas the tools they need to lift themselves out of poverty and into a better life. Together, we can build a society where everyone has the resources to thrive economically. Recreate differently and Restructure paraphrase without altering the quality and message within. "We can build efforts to lift people out of poverty and into more prosperous living situations if we value diversity, encourage collaboration between diverse sectors, and ensure everyone has access to fundamental requirements. We can build a better future by having honest conversations and working together across government, industry, and nonprofit sectors. Keeping this in mind, let's work together to end global poverty by promoting acceptance and cooperation. If we work together, we can change the world.

CHAPTER EIGHT

ETHICAL CONSIDERATIONS FOR WEALTH CREATION

As defined by the dictionary, the concept of riches encapsulates abundant resources. In the realm of monetary wealth, it denotes a substantial accumulation of financial assets, and pursuing this accumulation forms the essence of the wealth-building process. The components of wealth are diverse, encompassing real estate, stocks, cash reserves, gold holdings, mutual fund investments, and more. Upon offsetting liabilities and debts, this conglomerate of assets culminates in calculating our net worth—a quantifiable expression of our financial standing.

Yet, delving into the domain of prosperity unravels a multifaceted perspective. The assessment of wealth is inherently contextual, tethered to individual aspirations and benchmarks. The measure of affluence is intrinsically intertwined with one's aspirational benchmark; if financial resources suffice to fulfill every long-held ambition, one can rightfully claim the mantle of affluence. The spectrum of dreams often extends from envisioning a lavish 4-BHK apartment in the heart of South Delhi to nurturing fantasies of owning an apple orchard amidst the picturesque landscapes of Shimla. These aspirations embody a spectrum of desires, each demanding substantial financial backing.

Realizing such dreams necessitates a considerable outlay of financial resources. Acquiring the means to transform these aspirations into reality requires strategic wealth augmentation. The journey toward fulfilling these aspirations is inherently aspirational, fueling the pursuit of greater financial prosperity.

If one's current fiscal status falls short of supporting these ambitions, the path ahead is clear: an intentional pursuit of wealth expansion. By actively working towards augmenting one's financial reserves, the prospect of eventually materializing cherished dreams comes into sharper focus. This tenacity to secure a better tomorrow propels individuals to embrace opportunities for wealth generation and enhancement.

In essence, the trajectories of wealth and prosperity intersect at the intersection of dreams and fiscal potential. They encapsulate the multifaceted journey of accumulating assets, not merely for the sake of accumulation but as a conduit to transforming dreams into tangible realities. From high-rise abodes in bustling urban centers to tranquil retreats amidst nature's bounty, each aspiration necessitates a wealth-building endeavor. The endeavor isn't solely about amassing monetary resources; it's about nurturing dreams, fortifying potential, and scripting one's journey toward a life of abundance.

Wealth Lifestyle

It might take time to realize how maintaining a healthy lifestyle might positively impact one's financial situation. Even so, there are many commonalities between these ideas. When you prioritize your emotional and physical health, you also invest in your growth and career. You also avoid potential medical expenses and lost wages associated with any diseases or injuries you might prevent. However, when people change their lifestyles to benefit their health, they are more likely to achieve other goals, such as spending less money and helping promote sustainable economic models like collaborative and circular economies.

A lot of individuals link exercise with the amount of time spent at a fitness center engaging in activities such as treadmill running or weightlifting. Nonetheless, altering your routine could enhance your physical and emotional state, reduce costs, and contribute to the preservation of the environment. Choose walking or cycling over driving to your workplace or school whenever possible. This choice will result in reduced expenses associated with fossil fuels such as gasoline or electricity. Irrespective of your age, the World Health Organization (WHO) advises that adults aged 18 to 64 involve themselves in a minimum of 2.5 hours of moderate-intensity physical activity every week.

Enjoy a healthy diet. Foods high in sugar, processed ingredients, or excess fat can be attractive at the grocery store but may not deliver the nutrition your body needs. Make a list of everything you need before you go grocery shopping to prevent spending more money than you planned. Markets are a great place to find fresh, in-season fruits and vegetables and unprocessed, unpackaged products that you can chop and peel yourself. You can eat healthier and more affordably by doing this.

Get some shut-eye. There have inevitably been mornings when you felt sleepy or grumpy even before you opened your eyes. The quantity and quality of your slumber may hold the key. Sleep deprivation impairs cognitive functions such as attention, focus, learning, and memory and may lead to poor judgment when money is at stake. In addition to negatively impacting your health, it also raises the likelihood of injuries and accidents occurring due to drowsiness, which may place a financial burden on your family due to, for example, hospital expenses or lost wages.

Stay true to your ideals. Developing a habit of discipline can aid in developing the aforementioned positive routines. Consistency can be a motivating factor in the pursuit of other goals as well, such as those related to health and fitness, financial planning, and personal development. One way to stay motivated and on track is to create a plan, such as a calendar marking the days you intend to exercise or a monthly budget to manage your resources better (and save money for holidays). Building the habit of saving money or exercising takes time and effort, just like eating right or exercising.

Practice moderate consumption. Engaging in detrimental actions like excessive alcohol or smoking can exhaust your financial reserves and reduce your lifespan. Such habits involve monetary outlays that hinder your overall earnings. That's not even factoring in the potential cost of medical care, lost wages, or other consequences that could arise from any resulting disease or dependence. It is feasible to practice sustainable consumption in the marketplace, contributing to societal and environmental well-being. Sustainable finance, including green and social bonds, are two examples of responsible investment products. A different approach is forming routines that help save natural resources, such as using second-hand apps to repurpose old electronics or cutting down on energy use at home or the workplace.

Promising Practices In The Workplace

The promotion of healthy lifestyles among employees is becoming increasingly important to businesses. In addition to assisting in the attainment of goals and the enhancement of production, it also contributes to the well-being of your employees and the retention or attraction of talent. Companies can reap benefits, such as increased employee engagement and improved bonds among colleagues, from initiatives like physical activity days at the workplace and discussions with specialists to raise awareness of the importance of caring for one's physical and mental health both inside and outside of the workplace, and first aid training. In a nutshell, productivity and revenue rise with a well-functioning team. Taking care of yourself both at work and outside of it can help you save money in the long run.

Making Money

Simply increasing one's income will not result in a greater net worth. To generate a second source of revenue, you must invest your savings. Wealth creation refers to the act of growing one's wealth by the investment of one's savings in ways that are consistent with one's financial objectives. More than picking the appropriate investment is needed; you also need to give your money a chance to develop. Investing young will allow you to take full advantage of compound interest. Those who begin investing young are better positioned to ride out market fluctuations and more easily achieve their financial objectives.

One more strategy to ensure you reach your wealth creation objective is investing more of your income as it grows. Salary employees like yourself often receive raises once every year. You can save a lot more money if you increase your monthly investments by the same amount yearly as your annual increment. Especially at the outset of your investment career, it is more important to focus on the amount you invest than the rate of return. Because everyone has their own unique set of circumstances, there is no one surefire method for becoming wealthy. Long-term investors, for instance, would be better served by equity-oriented investments rather than debt-oriented ones. Debt and hybrid mutual funds, on the other hand, are better suited to short- and medium-term objectives.

Warren Buffet, a famed investor, once said, "If you don't find a way to earn money while you sleep, you will have to work till you die." This quote perfectly encapsulates the importance of wealth generation. One of the main goals of wealth creation, as he saw it, was the capacity to build wealth passively through the investment of money obtained in the past. In this approach, a person's wealth might increase steadily as time passes.

Creating wealth entails, at its core, growing one's money to meet numerous short-, intermediate-, and long-term monetary objectives. Saving for a trip or a new iPhone could be examples of short-term financial goals. These are short-term objectives, having a target completion date of three years or fewer. Typically, investments with a time frame of three to five years are considered medium-term aims. Saving for a car or a housing down payment are two good examples of goals that will help you build wealth.

However, the investing horizon for long-term goals, like having enough money saved for retirement, can be several years or even decades away. In this instance, you need to save enough money while working to cover your expenses once you retire. It's important to remember that your wealth creation goals and periods may be different, necessitating a range of approaches. You, as an investor, may have several opportunities to choose from. However, just as each tool in a toolbox is best suited for a different job, each investment strategy is best suited for another type of project. The security of the cash invested must be prioritized over the possible returns if, for instance, you are saving for a financial goal that you need to accomplish within six months.

For this reason, short-term investments should be made in low-volatility choices such as liquid funds or fixed deposits. However, if you want to succeed financially in the long run, you must put the growth of your investments ahead of their security. This error manifests itself frequently when people try to save for far future events like retirement or a house by choosing fixed return assets like Fixed Deposits (F.D.s) rather than Equity-oriented options like Flexicap Funds. Even though F.D. returns are guaranteed to be stable throughout the investment period, this type of investment is inappropriate for this situation. Therefore, it will require far more work on your behalf if you try to use only fixed-return instruments for long-term wealth growth. That's why tailoring your investing strategy to your unique needs for growing your money is essential. You may have several different financial objectives in mind at once.

There will only be retirement-level objectives among them. You may need to increase your savings for a new car or a home down payment. You'll be willing to take more or less risk on some goals than others, depending on how soon or far away they are. Therefore, you cannot trust a singular investment strategy to keep you on pace to accomplish all these objectives.

Consequently, you'll need to employ various wealth-creation tactics, each of which should be tailored to a specific set of financial objectives. You can diversify your holdings across local Equity, debt, international Equity, and gold with a mix of index funds, gold ETFs, and debt mutual funds, depending on the portfolio approach you select. E.T. Money Genius's algorithm will calculate the appropriate allocation of your investment portfolio depending on your wealth growth objective. You no longer need to spend time and energy picking investments and determining the proper asset allocation to achieve your financial goals.

The Genius algorithm will employ dynamic and strategic asset allocation tactics to schedule your entry into, and exit from different investments via one-tap monthly rebalancing, as your portfolio's allocation to multiple asset classes cannot remain static. Adapting your investing strategy regularly to suit shifting market conditions puts you in the best position to maximize profits while limiting losses during market downturns. Creating wealth is an ongoing procedure. If you want to accomplish your goals, you must create a strategy and stick to it. Furthermore, there is no one-size-fits-all approach to wealth generation due to differences in objectives, risk tolerance, etc. Attaining enduring financial prosperity significantly relies on making intelligent investment choices that propel you toward your goals.

Building Wealth

Building wealth is a gradual and consistent journey. Although the allure of overnight millionaire status might attract numerous individuals, the truth remains that rapid wealth accumulation usually stems from speculation, inheritance, or winning a lottery, with no sustainable path. The paradox of "rapid" wealth creation is that the slowest method for long-term success is the safest method. The underlying magic of amassing wealth lies in the compounding effect, which grows larger and larger the more quickly you can save and invest.

Here are ten methods to increase your wealth swiftly without taking unnecessary risks:

- **Save**

Without starting capital, wealth creation strategies are doomed to fail. Make saving money your number one priority as soon as you start earning money. Financial experts propose "paying yourself first," or saving a portion of each paycheck before covering other expenses. You will have to reduce your discretionary spending to make room for these "forced savings," but your wealth will increase quickly.

- **Invest in an S&P 500 Index Fund**

Relying on the S&P 500 index doesn't guarantee profits, yet its historical track record demonstrates significant gains for investors. The stock market, often perceived as risky, has never incurred losses over any continuous 20-year period, a fact that surprises many. Over the years, the S&P 500 has consistently delivered an average annual return of over 10%. This remarkable performance showcases the index's exceptional risk-to-reward ratio over the long run. Warren Buffett, the renowned investor known as the "Oracle of Omaha," has directed his trustee to allocate 90% of his wealth into an S&P 500 index fund.

Purchase stocks that provide dividends. Although investing in dividend-paying stocks may appear like a time-consuming and uninteresting way to build wealth, it is one of the finest methods to acquire access to a reliable and expanding source of income and capital gains. "Dividend Aristocrats" are S&P 500 index-listed companies that have regularly increased their dividend distributions for at least 25 years.

Recognizable names like Coca-Cola and McDonald's are counted among these esteemed companies. That means the people who bought these businesses 25 years ago are reaping enormous effective dividends. The Dividend Aristocrats can be an excellent strategy to amass wealth when dividends are factored in with the possibility of capital gains.

- **Invest in a Rental Home**

Earning passive income is a vital strategy for rapid and sustainable wealth accumulation. And owning a rental property (or properties) is a great method to produce passive income. You can count on a reliable monthly income from a well-managed rental property, and you won't have to lift a finger to make it happen. Your revenue will be self-sustaining once renters are in place and you've taken care of any necessary upkeep. Since rentals tend to go up over time and mortgage payments tend to go down, you can sit back and watch your properties appreciate while your renters pay off your mortgage.

- **You Should Never Stop Asking for Pay Raise**

Your experience and worth to your employer increase nearly every year, as does the expense of living. Therefore, you shouldn't be reluctant to request salary increases frequently to combat the effects of inflation and ensure that you are compensated fairly. You shouldn't be a pay negotiator, but you should make the case to your supervisor when it's warranted that your worth warrants a raise. Don't ignore this potential source of income creation; those who don't ask for raises typically don't get them.

- **Launch an Enterprise**

Most of the world's billionaires become wealthy through either inheritance (which is less of a strategy than pure good fortune) or the creation of their successful businesses. Creating and growing a prosperous business is one of the most likely ways to amass a substantial fortune. Of course, starting a business is a gamble, as many do not survive their initial few years in operation. This is a risky endeavor, but it can pay off handsomely if you develop a profitable company plan, secure adequate financing, and hire competent employees.

- **Broaden Your Background and Experience**

If you plan on spending your life in service to others, you might as well increase your worth as much as possible, right? One of the finest ways to show your worth to an employer is to continue your education and build a wide range of skills. If you want to increase your wealth, you should concentrate on developing specific skill sets in great demand, such as those in the well-paying I.T. and finance industries.

- **Create several Sources of Income**

Even with diligent saving, it can be challenging for one person to amass significant wealth from a single income. Create several different revenue streams to amass money quickly. You may, for instance, supplement your regular income by taking on a side gig that plays to your strengths. Broadening your client base is in your best interest if you're a freelancer. This will provide you with supplementary income and shield you from financial hardship if you lose your primary source of support during times of economic uncertainty.

- **Make Do With What You've Got**

Building wealth is unattainable if your expenses match your earnings. Formulating and sticking to a budget holds paramount importance. Suppose you aspire to secure long-term financial prosperity along with your regular spending, set aside a sizeable chunk of your budget for savings and investing. You may gradually accumulate wealth by lowering your monthly spending.

- **Don't Play It Safe**

While excessive risk-taking might cause you to lose everything you've worked for financially, excessive conservatism can have the same negative effect by preventing you from growing financially. You need to be willing to take some financial risks, such as investing more aggressively or starting your firm, if you want to amass enormous riches. After factoring in taxes and inflation, an investor who puts all their money into Treasury bills, for instance, will lose money. Investments with better return potential can be gained through stock ownership, property ownership, business ownership, and even cryptocurrency ownership. You should be aware that speculation can help you get rich but also exposes you to more risk.

Exploring Gender Differences in Access to Wealth Creation Opportunities

The gender wealth gap, or the female-to-male ratio of median wealth, is a less well-studied topic than the gender income gap, even though wealth inequality is even larger than income inequality. To calculate a family's wealth or net worth, we must subtract all their debts from their assets. The Labour and Liberal Democrat election manifestos strongly emphasize closing the gender wage gap, but this hotly argued economic and social issue has a more covert and rarely acknowledged sibling. Closing the "gender wealth gap" in the United Kingdom would boost women's economic autonomy and safety. What matters more than women's salaries is what they do with their money. Women make wiser financial decisions than males.

According to numerous researches, women investors have been shown to outperform men, ranging from 1.8% to 0.94 %. A contributing factor is that male investors are more likely to choose high-risk, speculative stocks. This is consistent with the widespread belief in the social and psychological sciences that males are inherently riskier than women, a theory now being challenged by studies revealing that risk preference is situational and learned rather than innate. Interesting as it may be, the U.K. has a gender investment imbalance of £15 billion. Compared to males, who have £29.3 billion in investments, women only have access to £14.3 billion. It's called the "investment gap" or "gender wealth gap" when this happens.

This trend emerged early on: only 4.4% of millennial women, compared to 7.3% of millennial males, currently own any financial product. In Generation X, the gap grows even further, with 16.1% of men investing compared to 9.6% of women. Differences in the usual saving habits of men and women contribute to the wealth divide. 892,000 women invested in government stocks and shares ISAs in 2015/16, the most recent year for which data is available, compared to 1.1 million men. During the same period, however, 1.2 million more women than men put money into cash ISAs, which are safer but offer far less return on investment.

Furthermore, studies have shown that people's saving habits may have roots in their formative years. Sixty-four percent of boys and only 54 percent of girls in a 2018 survey of 500 children reported chatting with their parents about money. Parents are more inclined to describe their sons as "clever with money" than their daughters are. These beliefs arise as a natural consequence of the sexism that permeates our culture's financial discourse. Sixty-five percent of money-related stories in women's magazines paint the gender as wasteful spenders, urging readers to rein in their spending by creating stricter budgets and less flexible spending limits rather than introducing the idea of investing. In contrast, seventy percent of men's magazines present financial success as a symbol of masculinity and celebrate the thrill of risk-taking. A lack of self-assurance is the long-term result of the social message, reinforced from early on, that women are "terrible" with money.

Only 13% of female investors and traders think they have a solid grasp of the stock market. Because of this doubt, many women avoid investing and store their cash in easy-access accounts. If you put £1 into such an account 10 years ago, you would have only 87 cents now. However, if the same pound had been invested in the FTSE 250 ten years ago, it would now be worth £2.53. In short, women do a great disservice by ignoring financial goods, no matter how much money they have stashed away. The good news is that it won't take much effort to close the wealth disparity between the sexes.

Compared to the gender pay gap, in which women and their wages are subject to negative external factors, the gender wealth disparity is largely within the control of individual women. It can be quickly reversed and doesn't necessitate massive institutional and social change like ending the gender wage gap. Some evidence suggests that people will start investing more once they better understand the potential benefits and threats associated with stock and share purchases. The government and the commercial sector should launch public awareness initiatives aimed at women to spark a national dialogue about the gender wealth gap and encourage more women to invest. We need to debate how to make women more financially secure, and that conversation needs to go beyond just discussing salaries.

Embracing a Culture of Inclusion and Collaboration

It's common knowledge that effective teams and businesses are built on a foundation of cooperation. And it's crucial in today's varied, dispersed, and globally connected workforce. Internally, businesses that foster a culture of cooperation see a rise in revenue, enhanced productivity, and new ideas. New products and services and improved internal operations can bring in more money and happier customers. Knowledge exchange and competence development among employees and contractors are other less obvious benefits. Collaboration is often incorrectly equated with terms like coordination, cooperation, and teamwork. However, you cannot just replace one term with another. Collaboration is the process of working together to improve upon an existing product or to address a difficult challenge. These assets could originate from anywhere (including outside the company), across groups, and in any number of physical places.

Creating prosperous nations requires actively fostering a culture of acceptance and cooperation. In today's interconnected global economy, the engagement of all citizens and the knowledge they possess are invaluable resources. Everyone in society benefits when conditions are fostered that encourage participation and cooperation. Respecting and valuing the diversity of thought is fostered, as it increases the amount of information available to the group. Because of this, new approaches to previously intractable issues become possible.

A culture that welcomes all people, regardless of ethnicity, gender, religion, age, or ability, fosters mutual respect. All these things help people feel more connected to one another and the world around them, which drives economic growth and creates wealth for nations. Better customer service and enhanced team chemistry are two further benefits that can accrue to businesses that actively promote a culture of acceptance and diversity. Businesses can learn from one another and advance the economy by maintaining open contact lines.

The government can help promote a culture of openness and cooperation by launching programs to increase communication between various groups. Some examples of such government-sponsored initiatives are mentoring programs and community-building events. By taking these measures, we can foster an environment of trust and togetherness that will help nations grow economically. Governments, organizations, and individuals can gain a deeper mutual understanding resulting from a more open and collaborative social climate. Encouraging dialogue and the resolution of differences can pave the way to a brighter future for all nations. An open and cooperative mindset might be considered an engine for economic growth.

To stimulate national economies, governments, corporations, and individuals must work together to foster an atmosphere of openness and cooperation. Taking this step will pave the way for better futures for people everywhere. By learning about one another, we can foster a culture of inclusivity and collaboration that will help nations grow in prosperity in the future. Today, you may make a difference by encouraging dialogue and accepting people of all ages, races, sexual orientations, religions, abilities, and physical states. Collectively, we hold the power to enact change and preserve lives. There exists the potential for organizations, nations, or even entities that could be viewed as rivals to collaborate harmoniously.

Our willingness and capacity to work together might be affected by our mindset. This is why taking stock of your motivations, assumptions, and habits is crucial to grow your ability to work well with others. Others believe it's detrimental to productivity to allow for multiple points of view in the workplace. We think conflict is healthy in collaborative organizations as long as disagreements remain professional and avoid getting personal. In reality, a plethora of viewpoints frequently results in a game-changing improvement. Your project's (and perhaps your business's) success hinges on your team's ability to work together despite their differences.

Protect and encourage trust. Show them how to act by doing so yourself. Be open and honest about your reasoning whenever possible to gain your team's trust. Make it clear that you see blunders not as setbacks but as teachable moments that can be dissected and improved together. Everyone wins when workers have a firm grasp on what is expected of them, room to try new things, and clear guidelines for success. It has the potential to facilitate easier workflows, clearer lines of communication, and fresh ideas. Include people in defining your mission, values, and objectives.

When formulating a mission statement (to inspire people to take action), a set of core values (to direct employees' actions), and long-term objectives, it's important to get feedback from a wide range of stakeholders (to focus energy). People won't be completely on board if these choices are decided solely by executives and pushed from on high without any input from the team. Participants tend to be more invested in the final product when allowed to voice their opinions. Involving people in these crucial decisions strengthens their dedication to the organization, team, or department.

Just be honest with one another. An open-door policy is a great way to foster impromptu communication between you and your staff as a collaborative leader. Encourage comments, questions, and suggestions. Pay close attention and listen carefully when they are speaking. Open out about what you know and urge others to do the same without worrying about being judged. Maintain openness, honesty, and dependability. Open and frank dialogue is essential to foster mutual regard and trust, essential to effective teamwork.

Gain and share your strength. Leaders who succeed early in their lives realize they need help from others to complete large-scale tasks. They need a group to think for themselves, take charge, and cooperate to succeed. When I think of a leader trying to go it alone, I see a crew team with only one oar in the water. One person rowing will only get you a little far, but with everyone pulling together, that boat will fly across the water. A truly collaborative culture results from leaders empowering their team while setting work direction, resolving issues, and removing roadblocks. The key to organizational success is creating an environment where people are encouraged to work together, but this will take time. It needs the backing of upper management and support from employees. Encourage your subordinates to work with others beyond their immediate team to foster a culture of cooperation. They will start to learn from one another, develop novel ideas, and perform at a better level, proving the adage that "none of us is as brilliant as all of us.

CONCLUSION

The elimination of global poverty is an ambitious but possible objective. We must be willing to pitch in and help the less fortunate. This entails seeing past superficial differences like socioeconomic status or color and realizing that everyone deserves equal access to necessities. We must also move beyond emergency response to prioritize efforts leading to lasting improvement. To ensure that everyone has the opportunity to make their own life and the lives of their family better, we need to collaborate on creating significant economic opportunities.

As a global community, we have the power to end global poverty if we work together toward that goal. By working toward this objective together, we can change the world so that everyone has a chance to live a dignified life. When you put your mind to something, nothing is impossible. As always, I appreciate you taking the time to read this.

Let's do something now to end global poverty. It's time right now! Your help is crucial to our efforts to end global poverty; please accept our sincere gratitude. Let's keep progressing toward our shared objective by consistently doing the little things that add to big things over time. No matter how big or small, our combined efforts can help us reach our goal of a society without poverty, where everyone has access to basic rights and a level of life befitting their dignity. We must always keep trying.

Reference

- Lulu (October 2023). Ending poverty. poverty/hardcover/product
- McAfee, M. (January 2018). Opportunity for whom? Building wealth through advancing racial equity.
- Lierse, H., Sachweh, P., & Waitkus, N. (2022). Introduction: Wealth, Inequality and Redistribution in Capitalist societies.
- Reinhardt, U. E. (July 2017). How businesses create wealth. Economic Blog.
- Hanna, J. B. a. T. (October 2019). Building Community Wealth through Community Resilience. San Francisco Fed
- Lumpkin, G. T., & Bacq, S. (2019). Civic Wealth Creation: A new view of stakeholder engagement and societal impact. Academy of Management Perspectives.
- Davidai, S. (2022). How do people make sense of wealth and poverty? Current Opinion in Psychology.
- Osypuk, T. L., Joshi, P., Geronimo, K., & Acevedo-García, D. (2014). Do social and economic policies influence wealth? A review. Current Epidemiology Reports.

- Ayres, R. U. (1988). Technology: The wealth of nations. Technological Forecasting and Social Change.
- Wiener, J. (December 2022). 11 Most effective wealth building strategies used by personal finance pros in 2023. The Kickass Entrepreneur.
- Napoletano, E. (July 2023). How To Build Wealth. Forbes Advisor.
- Hayes, A. (February 2023). Principles of building wealth. Investopedia.
- Bhasin, T. (October 2023). Wealth Creation: meaning, importance, and Strategies. Learn About Investment Tax Saving, and Financial Planning.
- Brar, K. (April 2023). How is Wealth Created? Role of Technology, Strategies, Barriers - Sukhbeer Brar. Sukhbeer Brar.
- Bhatt, N. (July 2020). 5 Long-term Strategies To Create Wealth. Entrepreneur.
- Wealth Daily. (May 2023). Wealth building tools: Essential Strategies for Financial success - Wealth Daily.
- Taylor, K. (October 2021). 5 easy ways to take control of your personal finances. Harvard Business Review.
- Basse, A. (November 2023). How to control of your finances: Easy steps you can take today. How to Be Rich.
- Belhaj, F. (February 2020). Why Wealthy Countries Must Step Up Their Contribution to Fight Global Poverty. World Bank.

- Wiener, J. (December 2022). 11 Most effective wealth building strategies used by personal finance pros in 2023. The Kickass Entrepreneur.
- Williams, G. (April 2022). 20 ways to make quick cash. US News & World Report.

- NerdWallet. (November 2023). 25 ways to make money online, offline and at home. NerdWallet.
- Solutions, R. (July 2023). 34 ways to make extra money. Ramsey Solutions.
- Cepf, S. A. (October 2023). Ways to make quick cash: 8 legitimate ways to earn quick cash now. Business Insider.
- Habits, B. M. (January 2023). How to start saving money: 8 money saving tips. Better Money Habits.
- Caballero RJ (1990) Consumption puzzles and precautionary savings. Journal of Monetary Economics
- Cloutier, R. (August 2023). How tax cuts affect the economy. Investopedia.
- Durante, A. (October 2023). Reviewing the impact of taxes on economic growth. Tax Foundation.
- Muley, R. (January 2016). Economic Effects of Taxation: Top 6 effects. Economics Discussion.
- McGurran, B. (August 2021). How to manage your debt. Experian.

- Garvey, J. (January 2020). How to prioritize debt and rebuild your credit.
- Beers, B. (April 2021). Should I pay off debt or invest extra cash?
- Loudenback, T. (2023, August 11). ETFs vs. Mutual Funds
- Chen, J. (October 2023). Exchange-Traded Fund (ETF) explanation with pros and cons.
- Danielsson, M. (2022, September 23). How to reach financial Freedom: 12 Habits to Get you there.
- Kerr, E. (September 2022). How to know if the 50/30/20 budget will work for you.
- Thomas, M. (June 2023). Invest Wisely: Why You Should Leverage Learning and Development Professionals To Shape Corporate Training.
- James Royal, Ph.D. (October 2023). How to start investing in cryptocurrency: A guide for beginners.
- Block, Z. and I.C. MacMillan (1993), Corporate Venturing: Creating New
- Skat-Rordam, P. and Muzyka, D.F. (1999), Changing Strategic Direction: Practical Insight into Opportunity Driven Business Development.
- Stevenson, H.H. and Jarillo-Mossi, J.C., (1986), Preserving Entrepreneurship as Companies Grow, Journal of Business Strategy.

- Tepstra, D.E. and Olson, P.D. (1993), Entrepreneurial Start-up and Growth: A Classification of Problems, Entrepreneurship Theory and Practice.
- Williams, D.L. (1999), Why do Entrepreneurs Become Franchisees: An Empirical Analysis of Organizational Choice, Journal of Business Venturing.
- Mourdoukoutas, P. (1999), Collective Entrepreneurship in a Globalising Economy, Welspatt, Connecticut.
- Hood, J.N. and Young, J.E. (1993), Entrepreneurship's Requisite Areas of Development: A Survey of Top Executives in Successful Entrepreneurial Firms, Journal of Business Venturing.
- Steinmueller, W. E. (2010) 'Economics of Technology Policy', in Hall, B. H. and Rosenberg, N. (eds.) Handbook of the Economics of Innovation.
- Schumpeter J (1934) The theory of economic development. Cambridge, MA: Harvard University Press.
- Rothwell, R. (1982) Government innovation policy: Some past problems and recent trends, Technological Forecasting and Social Change
- Nelson, R. R. and Winter, S. G. (1982) An Evolutionary Theory of Economic Change, Cambridge, Mass: Harvard University Press.
- Corporation, T. E. H. (November 2023). Supporting education, research and development for wealth creation.
- Hub, G. I. (November 2021). The vital role of infrastructure in economic growth and development.

- Vagliasindi, M. (October 2023). How does infrastructure support sustainable growth? World Bank.
- Edwina. (February 2022). Developing strategic approaches to infrastructure planning. ITF.
- Rocky, T. (2019). Sources of Long-term Financing. Jkkniu.
- Mahembe, E., & Odhiambo, N. M. (2019). Foreign aid and poverty reduction: A review of international literature. Cogent Social Sciences.
- Duncan, Duncan, & Duncan. (September 2022). 9 Ways Foreign aid reduces poverty. Humanitarian Careers - LAUNCH YOUR CAREER IN HUMANITARIAN AID.
- Bhasin, M. L. (n.d.). Economic Value Added and Shareholders' Wealth Creation: Evidence from a Developing Country
- Fernando, J. (September 2023). Gross domestic product (GDP): formula and how to use it.
- Pettinger, T. (March 2022). Difference between GNP, GDP and GNI. Economics Help.

Published By: THE AGELESS PRESS

contact@theagelesspress.com

Made in the USA
Monee, IL
12 November 2026

bad8019f-739e-488e-b604-3da0540cf58fR01